MW01615481

BLACK MASCULINITY

BLACK MASCULINITY

The Black Male's Role in American Society

ROBERT STAPLES

THE**BLACK**SCHOLAR Press

Acknowledgments

Several of the chapters of this book were originally published as essays in THE BLACK SCHOLAR. Chapter 1 was originally published under the title "Masculinity and Race: The Dual Dilemma of Black Men," in the *Journal of Social Issues,* Vol. 34, No. 1, and is reprinted here by permission.

No part of this book may be reproduced or transmitted in any form by any means, without written permission of the publisher.

Copyright © 1982 by Robert Staples

Fourth Printing, 1984

All rights reserved

LC #81-69452

ISBN # 0-933296-06-1 (softcover)
       0-933296-07-X (hardcover)

Printed in the United States of America

Published by The Black Scholar Press,
P.O. Box 7106,
San Francisco, CA 94120.

305.38
St 27b

Dedication

For My Sisters,
Betty and Ella,
and
My Aunt and Uncle,
Cora and Winston McGill,
who helped shape my
own masculinity.

CONTENTS

INTRODUCTION

It is difficult to think of a more controversial role in American society than that of the black male. He is a visible figure on the American scene, yet the least understood and studied of all sex-race groups in the United States. His cultural image is usually one of several types: the sexual superstud, the athlete, and the rapacious criminal. That is how he is perceived in the public consciousness, interpreted in the dominant media and ultimately how he comes to see and internalize his own role. Rarely are we exposed to his more prosaic role as worker, husband, father and American citizen. Even when he might be applauded for acts of heroism, as in the disproportionate number of black men who served in the Vietnam war, public approbation eludes him because the war effort was both criminal and unsuccessful.

The following essays focus on the stereotypical roles of black males, not to reinforce them, but to penetrate the superficial images of black men as macho, hypersexual, violent and exploitative. Obviously, there must be sought some explanation for the dominance of black men in the nation's negative statistics on crime, unemployment, war, divorce, etc. Thus, my essays might be seen as an effort to explore the reality behind the image. For pedagogical purposes, the topics might be organized into crime and violence, male sexuality, male/female relationships and sex roles in the black community. If the reader wants to know the author's perspective or ideology, it is based on conflict theory. This perspective embraces some elements of Marxist, Pan-Africanist and internal colonialism models.

As a starting point, I see the black male as being in conflict with the normative definition of masculinity. This is a status which few, if any, black males have been able to achieve. Masculinity, as defined in this culture, has always implied a certain autonomy over and mastery of one's environment. It can be said that not many white American males have attained this ideal either. Yet, white males did achieve a dominance in the nuclear family. Even that semblance of control was to be largely denied the black man. During slavery he could receive the respect and esteem of his wife, children and kinsmen. But, he had no formal legal authority over his wife and children. And, there are numerous and documented instances of the attempts of the slave owning class to undermine his respect and esteem in the eyes of his family.

Beginning with the fact that slave men and women were equally subjugated to the capricious authority of the slaveholder, the African male saw his masculinity challenged by the rape of his woman, sale of his children, the rations issued in the name of the woman and children bearing *her name* — while his presence went unrecognized. Those practices may have presaged the beginning of a healthier sexual equalitarianism than was possible for whites, but they also provoked contradictions and dilemmas for black men in American society. While parity between men and women may be a current societal goal, among some segments of the society, it was hardly the American ideal in the nineteenth century. Instead it led to the black male's self-devaluation qua man and set the stage for internecine conflict within the black community.

Sex role identity is crucial to a person's values, life-style and personality. Black men have always had to confront the contradiction between the normative expectations attached to being male in this society and the proscriptions on their behavior and achievement of goals. Surely, this has psychological ramifications which have yet to be explored or understood. Instead, he is subjected to societal opprobrium for failing to live up to the standards of manhood on the one hand and for being super macho on the other. It is a classical case of "be damned if you do and damned if you don't." In the past there was the assertion that black men were effeminate because they were raised in households with only a female parent or one with a weak father figure. Presently, they are being attacked in the literature, in plays, and at conferences as having succumbed to the male chauvinist ideal.

In the decade of the eighties, black males may prove to be the first, perhaps only, casualty, of the women's movement. Without being in opposition to that movement, it is necessary to recognize that it can not be mechanically transferred to the black community. It is the prevailing notion of women qua victims that has led, rightfully so, to the increased societal attention to their concerns and problems. Yet, in the black community, it is the men who need attending to. They are the ones who are failing in school, losing ground in the labor market to white and black women, filling up the prisons and dying slowly through drugs, alcohol, violence and adventurism.

Ultimately, black women, too, become victims of the problems black men face. For the foreseeable future, most black women will have some kind of involvement with black men. They will suffer at the hands of narcotized, abusive black males, who are poorly educated, without skills, unable to obtain employment or contribute to the support of a family. When the statistics show that 85 percent of all black college graduates are women, it will be black women bemoaning the lack of men on their level to marry. Indeed, it is not the question of sexual parity that the black community will face in the future, but how it will adjust to female educational and economic superiorty. As long as we live in a society which preaches equality between the sexes but operates on the assumption that men are more equal, a group which assimilates those values will have problems when its economic arrangements are out of line with the dominant cultural patterns.

Despite the foregoing statements I am concerned about the problems and rights of black women. This book does not focus very much on those problems and concerns for reasons that should be obvious to the reader. Basically, I am concerned here with the problems of black men. The careful reader will note that I have no anti-black female perspectives. Those who hold to a rigid and feminist ideology of women qua victim have been quick to jump to the opposite conclusion. Any meticulous reading will detect that I have been critical of black men for their unmitigated male chauvinism. Still I have attempted to temper my criticism with an explanation and understanding of their behavior. Hopefully, what results is a balanced view of the black male's role in American society.

This book on black masculinity is the second in a trilogy on age and sex roles in the black family. Already, I have dealt with the sexual, marital and familial roles of black women. At this time there exists no book, single authored, that has examined the role of black men in the United States. This is a long overdue book since it is very difficult to understand the role of black females without understanding the role of black men. Much of the material in this book has been published elsewhere in a considerably different form. All of the previously published chapters have undergone some revision. Where possible, I have updated statistics and used recent studies. The basic purpose of this book is to examine the multiple dimensions of the role of black males in American society.

Part I:
Black Men
and the Social System

CHAPTER ONE

Race and Masculinity:
The Dual Dilemma of Black Men

In recent years a great deal of attention has been given to the role of black women and their super-oppressed status in American society. This emphasis on black women was generated by the women's liberation movement and highlighted the domination of the society by men and the subordinate role of women.[1] Most of the literature has focused on the privileges of masculinity in gaining access to the values and goals of the culture. Males have begun to question themselves, their own sex-role expectations and to assess the negative consequences, as well as the advantages of their gender.

In the case of black men, their subordination as a racial minority has more than cancelled out their advantages as males in the larger society. Any understanding of their experience will have to come from an analysis of the complex problems they face as blacks and as men. Unlike white males, they have few privileges in this society except vis-à-vis black women, and even that advantage is being eroded by black women who have a competitive edge over some black males for certain jobs. Indeed, in comparison to white males, black men find themselves on the negative side of social statistics in the area of health, employment, education, income, etc. As a result, we have to examine the sociocultural forces which have combined to create the increasing plight of black men in the United States.

The experiences of males and females — black and white — in their lives are critical and different from each other. Black men face certain problems related to institutional racism and environments

7

which often do not prepare them very well for the fulfillment of masculine roles. In addition to the problems created by institutional and overt discrimination, they encounter the negative stereotyping that exists on all levels about them: being socially castrated, insecure in their male identity, and lacking in a positive self-concept. Most of these negative stereotypes have been perpetuated by the social science literature, and have stemmed from a failure to understand the meaning and form of masculinity in black culture and as a result of the application of white norms to black behavior.

In the pre-slave era, blacks lived in what can only be described as a patriarchal society on the African continent. It does not appear to have generated the total submission of women as was true of comparable European cultures. There are numerous cases where women in Africa exceeded their European counterparts in their authority and contribution to their respective social units.[2] Until recently, it had been assumed that slavery destroyed all vestiges of a black patriarchy by its suppression of the bondsman's authority over his family. The work of historian Stanley Elkins gave rise to a number of other theories that depicted the black man as a docile personality whose will had been broken by slavery.[3] More recent historical research has presented us with a more balanced portrait of the male slave. Alex Haley's book, *Roots*, and the popular television production of that work most vividly illustrates the strong and resistant role of black men during the slavery era.[4]

There were a variety of responses to the coercive institution of slavery. They ranged from the grinning, shuffling "Sambo" of pro-slavery lore to the revengeful runaways to many who used guile and humor to escape from work or to manipulate the slave owner.[5] It is impossible to determine which response was dominant, only that all black men did not respond uniformly to the same condition. A theory concomitant with the Elkins' thesis was that under slavery black men abdicated their responsibility to their families.[6] Subsequent historical research has shown that most slave households had a male as head who fulfilled certain role prerequisites under the limited autonomy possible in a total institution. The fact that men did not have unlimited authority in the family, according to Genovese, was "in fact a closer approximation to a healthy sexual equality than was possible for whites."[7]

After slavery officially ended, the kind of role flexibility that existed during slavery continued for black families. Despite theories to the contrary, male-present households were the norm in poor black communities in the period between 1880–1925. Families headed by women were hardly, if at all, more common than among comparable whites.[8] These two-parent black households were often dual-worker families, as many wives worked alongside their husbands in order to obtain land and an education for their children. It was out of the harsh economic conditions of the late nineteenth century that a certain egalitarianism developed within the black families, and the sharp dichotomy between male and female sex roles, so common to antebellum Southern white families, failed to develop.

THE MYTH OF THE MATRIARCHY

Although one-parent households have always been a minority of all black families, a number of assumptions have been made about their influence on the acquisition of male identity patterns for the boys lodged in such households. Such notions have more relevance today since a near majority of black children presently live in female-headed households.[9] Those who argue that male children can not learn the content of their masculine roles make the erroneous supposition that there are no male role models available from whom those children can learn. In her study of matricentric households, Stack notes the striking fact that households almost always have men around: male relatives, in-laws, and boyfriends. Children have constant and close contact with these men and their relationships last over the years.[10]

The fact that many black women head households has resulted in the stereotype of black men as castrated by their women, who have gained ascendency in the family through their greater education and economic contribution. Even in families where the husband is present, the wife is alleged to be the dominant figure in decision making. These pejorative stereotypes have persisted because black families are generally more equalitarian than comparable white families. Because of sexism in this society, few black women earn more than their husbands. Even in low-income families, 85 percent of the husbands have a higher income than the wife.[11] Most black wives are not dominant matriarchs but share with their husbands the making of family decisions. With the special problems black women face — such as early pregnancies, the burdens of supporting children alone, and inadequate incomes and job opportunities — it is difficult to imagine them as having castrated the slightly better-off male.

Alongside these stereotypes of the black male extant in the social science literature is the lingering one of his negative self-concept, a subjective devaluation that derives from labelling processes in the family and his inferior status in the larger society. While this could be the logical outcome of minority status in this society, counter-vailing forces operate to maintain a high level of self-esteem for most black males. Among these forces is the insider-outsider dichotomy in selecting reference groups as guides for the expected level of achievement. Instead of using the standards of the white majority group, many black males measure their worth by the achievement of others within their own culture. Being a member of an oppressed minority group also allows individual members to be extrapunitive in determining the reasons for their failures in life.[12] Despite notions to the contrary, positive experiences in their families do serve as a source of positive self-identity for the develop-ing male child.[13]

SOCIALIZATION INTO MANHOOD

As is true of majority youth, blacks have a variety of socializing agents and institutions upon which to draw for their male identity. Being exposed to the school, family, mass media, and peer group means that a number of different values and roles are being con-veyed to them at any point in time. Family structure and socio-economic status are considered key factors in determining the kind of role models presented to the growing child. We have already noted the dominant — but unproven — theory that the content of the male role is not adequately conveyed to black youth because of absent or weak father figures. This ignores the fact that black boys learn the male role from a variety of sources. Even if there were not strong male role models available, women are able to transmit the male sex-role expectations symbolically, e.g., telling them how to walk, to carry their books, etc.

These children, however, are depicted as having different problems. It is not that they are unexposed to male role models, but the male role models present negative images of manhood and achievement to impressionable male children. Examples of such negative role images would be the pimp and hustler in low-income ghettos, who are the only successful men to whom many young boys are exposed. While this is a salient and somewhat valid point, it overlooks the fact that the pimp and hustler prototypes exist primarily in large Northern cities and are rare in the smaller towns and in the South. Moreover, as Taylor has noted, role model identifications can be observed to be closely related to the dominant concerns of youth at that time. What this means is that youth who are interested in a career, in developing interpersonal skills, or are preoccupied with a social or political issue focus on those environmental models assumed to be relevant and useful toward the resolution of those concerns.[14]

It is difficult to single out a dominant force in the socialization process for black youth. The complexity of our society is such that they will be exposed to a number of models. Several key studies indicate that family background is an important — if not decisive — factor which influences the masculinity of young black males. For example, Benjamin discovered that male youths had a better conception of the socially accepted and prescribed model of the male familial role when their fathers had one or more years of college education. The implication of his finding is that a strong association exists between the opportunity to play a role and the actual playing of that role.[15]

Questions might be raised about the tendency of many black youth to associate masculinity with hypersexuality and violence. It is true that many black youth are socialized and exposed to violence in their environments and in the mass media. Whether this becomes their only concept of masculinity depends on the opportunity to fulfill other concepts of masculinity. Violence as a means of status conferral will continue to exist among black youths in the underclass as long as the opportunity structure for other expressions of their masculinity remains blocked by the forces of institutional racism. This is in reality a class, not a racial determination, and exists among lower-class groups of all races.[16]

PROBLEMS OF THE YOUNG BLACK MAN

Strongly related to the issue of black masculinity are the problems encountered on the path to manhood. Few Americans are unaware of the presence of young black men and they are generally regarded as a source of tension in the social structure. First, they are a large and quite visible group, particularly in the inner city, relative to the total black population. Over 54 percent of the black population is under 24 years of age, compared to only 45 percent of whites.[17] Secondly, they are over-represented in the statistics on violent crimes, a phenomenon which has many Americans in a state of terror. What has happened to this group of young black males cannot be explained in simplistic terms of poor parenting or innate racial traits. It is the persistence of barriers to the expression of the masculine role that best explains their antisocial behavior.

The high school dropout rate is 25 percent for blacks in contrast to 15 percent for whites.[18] This means that many black youth are without educational credentials or job skills and experience. The net result of this statistic is a 40 percent jobless rate for black males in the central cities.[19] Unofficial, but no less authoritative, surveys of black teenage unemployment put the figure at close to 70 percent.[20]

What this means in very real terms is that the work function so closely associated with masculinity in this society is denied to the majority of black male youths. One finds a close correspondence between the joblessness of black male youths and their behavior patterns. This finds its most vivid manifestation in the crime statistics that show the largest number of crimes against a person and acts of theft were committed by black males below the age of 24. The largest group responsible for homicides in this country is that of black males in the 20- to 24-year age range. And their victims are similarly young black men — a fact which has as its most tragic consequence that homicide is listed as the number one cause of death among black males aged 15–30. If there is any doubt that these young black men are members of the underclass, it can be relieved by the statistic which shows that almost 60 percent of young black prison inmates reported an annual income of less than $3,000.[21]

Not all of the response to failure to fulfill their manhood is expressed in antisocial behavior. Some of it is aggression turned inward. In New York City the highest cause of death among black youths is narcotic addiction. Another symptom of their feelings of powerlessness and hopelessness is a suicide rate among black youths that is higher than that of the total population of all ages. Others may seek to escape the fate of the criminal, the drug addict, and the suicide victim by joining the ranks of the volunteer army. More than a third of the new recruits into the volunteer army were young black men.[22]

It is patently clear that the central concerns of black men are not about relinquishing male privilege or forging new concepts of androgyny or sex-role egalitarianism. They must first and foremost deal with the issue of survival. It is not that they have abused the privileges accruing to men, but that they have never been given the opportunity to realize even the minimal perquisites of manhood — life-sustaining employment and the ability to support a family. To a large extent, these problems are confined to a certain segment of the black population, but they constitute a very large proportion of all black men. We should also realize that the more these legitimate aspirations to manhood are retarded, the greater the tendency will be to assert them in other areas.

ROLE ASCRIPTION AND FULFILLMENT

Within the youth period, attitudes are formed toward futuristic life styles and roles; hence it is necessary to assess how young black males see themselves — if at all — in the roles of lover, husband, and father. Are the roles of husband and father subordinate to the more glamorous and mass-media portrayed ones of the free-wheeling bachelor and super-stud? We need to analyze the role priorities among black men, and the forces in their environment which facilitate or impede their fulfillment.

Lovers and Sexual Consorts

Folklore and research both depict the black male as preoccupied with his role as a lover and sexual partner. The concept of black male hypersexuality dates as far back as the sixteenth century, when Englishmen described Africans as beset by an unrestrained

lustfulness[23]. Until recently, the trait of black male sexual competency was pejoratively viewed as the sexuality of beasts and the
bestiality of sex. A less racist conception of black male sexuality is
that it is a secondary symbol of manhood in a society that denies
him the primary signs of masculinity, such as high status jobs.[24]
Psychiatrists Grier and Cobbs have suggested that it is a symbol of
power employed as an armament and used as a cautious and
deliberate weapon against whites.[25]

Such ascriptions of underlying motives and drives ignore the
normative sexual socialization patterns of black men in this society.
They, as well as females, are very early socialized into heterosexual
relations by their culture and extended family system. A sexual
orientation is well inculcated long before they become aware of the
constraints on their other expressions of masculinity. Less rigid age
and sex roles in the black community expose them at an early age
to a more permissive sexual ethos. Because the restraints placed on
black female sexual expressions have not been as severe as for her
white counterpart, black male sexuality has been liberated and has
provided a greater opportunity structure for sexual contacts. It is
only in a puritanical culture such as exists in the United States that
male sexual interest is viewed with the disapprobation imposed on
black males.

There is little doubt that black men are the most liberal of the
sex-race groups. They start dating earlier, are more likely to have a
romantic involvement in high school, have the most liberal sexual
attitudes, and are most inclined to have non-marital sex without
commitment.[26] This does not mean that they have no sexual standards, but only that the ones they have are less conservative than
those of other sex-race groups. In particular there is a double standard in regard to what women should be allowed to do.[27] It should
be noted that their double standard has not been as rigid or as oppressive as that of many white males. Black women are not labelled
as "good" or "bad" girls on the basis of virginity or nonvirginity, but
discretion in sexual affairs is expected, as is sexual exclusivity in a
relationship where the male has an emotional investment.

Charges of black male hypersexuality have often come from
white males, for reasons that many think are suspect. The sexual
prowess of black men, whether true or not, has been seen as a

threat to the powerful status of the white male in this society. Such fears have been symbolically manifested in attempts to castrate black men as part of the lynchings and other acts of terror against them. This led Clark to suggest: "The white man in America has, historically, arranged to have both white and Negro women available to him. He has claimed sexual priority with both, and, in the process he has sought to emasculate Negro men."[28] Others believe that black men still pose a sexual threat to white manhood although most whites would probably not admit it.[29] One sociological experiment demonstrated that even liberal white males can be rankled to violence by the hint of black sexual competition.[30]

Husbands

Clearly, the role of husband implies more responsibility and requires more than the role of lover and sexual consort. Black men who face uncertain futures see marriage as a risky undertaking. At an early age, many decide that they never want to take on the risk of marriage or be subjected to its requirements. This reluctance to marry is obviously associated with income and employment potential. Only 55 percent of black men earning less than $1,000 a year marry, in comparison to 80 percent of those earning between $3,000–$5,000. As incomes rise so do the number of black men who marry.[31] The fears of lower-class black men are rooted in an objective reality. They also have the highest divorce rate of any segment of the black population.[32]

While they may fear the responsibilities of marriage and the possibility of failure, black men do have an egalitarian attitude toward that institution. As early as adolescence, they expect egalitarian marriage roles concerning authority, housekeeping, and care of children. In comparison to white males, black husbands are more accepting of a wife's employment outside the home. Studies of familial decision-making processes reveal that black marriages are as egalitarian — or unegalitarian — as white ones. Where differences were found, they were related more to class than race. In general, blue-collar husbands of both races exercised more power in decisions in such areas as recreation, joint purchases, and household tasks than their white collar counterparts.[33]

Fathers

The role of father is a vexatious one for many men in this society. It is a role that is ill-defined in terms of its function and, to many people, mostly means economic support of the growing child. Whatever the definition, it is evident that the physical care and socialization of children is a task that women primarily perform. While women are assigned the basic caretaker role for children, men often define their masculinity in terms of the ability to impregnate women and to produce many children, especially sons who are regarded as extensions of themselves. For many lower-income black males, there is an inseparable link between their self-image as men and their ability to have sexual relations with women and the subsequent birth of children from those sexual acts. At the root of this virility cult is the lack of role fulfillment available to men of the underclass. The class factor is most evident here if we note that middle class black males sire fewer children than any other group in this society.[34]

Once he has sired children, the black father is then faced with the problem of supporting them as well as helping them to cope with environmental forces. Neither of these tasks is very easy for a class of men subjected to sporadic periods of unemployment and low wages at jobs they do obtain. Some black men deal with this painful psychological dilemma by abdicating the official responsibility of fatherhood and leaving the home. Liebow found that some men found it easier to show concern and gentleness with the children of women with whom they were cohabiting, since they did not have to fear failure and feelings of guilt, as was true of children to whom they had normatively defined obligations.[35] However, many low-income fathers do maintain contact with their children and carry out normal paternal functions. Stack reports that a mother generally regards her children's father as a friend of the family whom she can recruit for help, rather than as a father failing his parental duties.[36]

When black fathers are not beset by economic difficulties, their role as fathers is often not as marginal as imagined. Those social scientists who have studied ordinary black fathers have found them to be significant others to their children. The black father is not simply a shadowy figure who provides them with money or metes out punishment. He is a frame of reference, the person in general most respected and admired, and the most likely to be emulated by the children. Scanzoni reports that the father was the male figure most admired by children of both sexes.[37] However, black children are not uncritically accepting of the male parent. His relevance to the child is often contingent upon what he does or fails to do for the child and upon his ability to provide critical resources such as teaching the child coping skills and general value orientations.[38] Middle class black fathers are more capable of providing these resources and, consequently, participate more in child care than do their white counterparts. They are very child-oriented, and view their roles as different from the mothers'.[39]

MALE SEXISM AND BLACK FEMINISM

Although black men represent one of the most powerless groups in America, this does not mean they are devoid of sexist feelings or practices. Their own lowly position has effectively prevented them from suppressing their women in the same manner that white males have dominated white females. They have been forced to adopt more egalitarian views towards the role of women as a result of certain historical and social forces. Moreover, as a result of the same intersection of forces, the gap in sex-role equality is not that great between black men and women. Not only is the disparity in income and occupational status less, but black women are actually better educated than black men at most levels.[40]

This, however, has not prevented black men from gaining ascendency over women by virtue of their gender. Despite having more education, black women consistently have a higher rate of unemployment and earn less income than black males. In addition, they suffer many of the liabilities of white women as a result of the pervasiveness of sexism in this society. The black woman is the victim of sexual stereotyping, is forced in many cases to bear the responsibility for family planning alone, and is expected to cater to male desires and to assume a subordinate role. Whereas her main concerns relate to the problems of racism and economic survival, she is becoming increasingly preoccupied with the problems of gender per se. As a result, we have witnessed a burgeoning of black feminist organizations to tackle women's issues.

Currently, black women are relatively uninvolved in the mainstream women's movement, but feminism as an ideology is beginning to take hold. It was manifest in the demands of coeds at predominantly black, all-female Spelman College that the new college president should be a black woman. It is symbolized in the manifesto of the National Black Feminist Organization:

> We will remind the Black Liberation Movement that there can't be liberation for half a race. We must, together, as a people, work to eliminate racism from without the Black Community which is trying to destroy us as an entire people, but we must remember that sexism is destroying and crippling us from within. [41]

Among the sexist acts they speak of are the subordinate roles black women are forced to play in black organizations and institutions, a practice best exemplified by the famous statement of a black civil rights leader that the black women's position in that movement "should be prone."

The black male's response to the above charge has been slow in forthcoming. To a large extent he believes, as do many white males, that the women's demand for equal rights is a threat to whatever masculinity he's been allowed by the larger society. There is some resentment, particularly among middle class black males, about what is considered the preferential treatment in jobs for black women who are used as a double minority in Affirmative Action hiring. For example, out of 28,500 broadcast officials and managers, the percentage of black men has remained constant at 2.3 percent while the percentage of black women in management positions has risen from 1 to 1.7 percent in the period between 1975 and 1979. [42] Obviously, developments such as these are forcing some changes in black male behavior. One notes a discernible erosion of the double sexual standard, more men participating in childcare and sharing of housework and domestic decisions. One factor retarding these changes in male behavior is the excess number of women over men in the black community. Because of the severe competition for the low pool of eligible black males, many black women are still forced to take marriage on male terms.

SUMMARY

In discussing the burden of masculinity and race for the black male, one has to assign priorities. It is quite clear that the problems caused by the legacy of racism are paramount. Although many middle class black males will have to concentrate on the changing role of women, black males of the working class must continue to confront the challenge of economic survival. It is questionable how much emphasis should be placed on reorienting their concept of traditional sex-roles when they, in many cases, have not been allowed equal access to those roles. Sex-role equality for the poorest of the poor is a meager victory at best. The machination of social forces has placed black men in a position where one-fourth are without jobs, they are the only sex-group whose life expectancy did not increase in the last decade, many are not keeping pace with the educational progress of other sex-race groups, and they have made less progress in white-collar areas relative to white males than black females have made relative to white females.

At the same time the changing role expectations of black women will necessitate some adjustments on the part of black males. These changes will be most pronounced in the middle class, since they have more resources to share, and it is among this group that the demands for sex-role equality will be heard. Such changes may be slow in coming due to countervailing forces. When men have a large pool of women to select from, they can afford to choose those who will conform to traditional sex-role norms; and women who are selecting from a limited pool of eligible males may opt to adhere to a subordinate role rather than do without. Many black women, however, will refuse to permit men to define black womanhood and will demand parity in the home and in all aspects of black life.

What will happen in the future is hard to determine. Many black men will continue to fall behind black women in their educational and economic progress. The result may be a black female dominance of high-status positions. Some segments of white society will be pleased with this result because they perceive black women to be less threatening to their racial hegemony. At the same time, large numbers of black women — and men — will continue to occupy the bottom levels of the socioeconomic strata. Whether either is better off than the other is an academic question; the need is for both black and women's liberation. The issues of masculinity and of race are too interwoven to separate at this time. What is necessary is a serious effort by this society to eliminate both racism and sexism from our lives.

CHAPTER TWO:

To Be Young, Black and Male

In American society the age of adolescence has often been a period of rebellion from parental dominance, and has been labelled *sturm* and *drang*. For white, middle class youths it was sometimes an age of frivolity characterized by indulgence in activities such as fraternity hazing, rock concerts or a brief flirtation with counter-culture behavior such as experimentation with drugs or alternative life styles. For young black men there was historically no such stage as adolescence, where one could be carefree until taking on the responsibilities of manhood. During the era of slavery, they were denied any childhood at all. As was true of their parents, they were forced into the fields to work, often as early as the age of seven. By the time they reached puberty, many were snatched away from their families and sold on the auction block.[1]

Not too much has changed for Afro-American youths since the official end of slavery. Far from enjoying the carefree period of adolescence, to find their adult identity, they have been forced into the labor market to become a commodity of exploitation by the power elite. To be young and black in the urban areas of the United States is to be subjected to all the harshest elements of oppression at the most vulnerable period of one's life. And, it is in the machinations of institutional racism that we see the future of black America, with the ranks of its young men, decimated by their role as a reserve labor force, military pawns and disruptive forces in the black community. The forces of capitalism threaten to make black male youth their primary victim. It is they who will suffer most from the oppressive role of the industrial order. As a group without

21

the psychological maturity of adults or the emotional shelter provided children, they are most vulnerable to the dynamics of racism
in its crudest form.[2]

If we define the period of youth as the ages between 16–24 years,
we can see how institutional racism functions successfully against
this important group of Afro-Americans. Because of a higher fertility rate, the proportion of black youth is higher than white youth
in this country. Approximately 54 percent of the Afro-American
population is under 24 years of age, compared to only 45 percent of
the white group.[3] This large number of young Afro-Americans is
central to the functioning of certain institutions such as the schools,
the military and the economy. As in classical colonial societies, the
use of young black males seems to increase the privileges which ac-
crue to members of the ruling group. We can best understand this
process by examining the oppression of Afro-American youths and
its affect on the political economy.

OPPRESSION OF AFRO-AMERICAN YOUTH
AND THE POLITICAL ECONOMY

As we have mentioned already, Afro-American youths are
catapulted early into the labor force because their income is needed
for the support of their families. These young men will usually be
without formal educational credentials or job skills and experience.
As a result they will have to accept the most menial or low-paying
jobs such as floor-washers, elevator operators, material handlers,
etc. These are also the jobs most easily mechanized and they are
quickly disappearing. A most obvious result of this economic reality is a very high unemployment rate among black youths. Among
black teenagers, for example, the official unemployment rate during the second quarter of 1980 was 40.3 percent, the highest jobless
rate of any group of workers in the United States. The similar rate
for white teenagers was 17.4 percent, considerably less.[4]

However, it has been shown in other surveys that the "real"
unemployment rate is sometimes three or four times higher than
the official unemployment figures. According to Dr. Bernard
Anderson, 65 percent of America's black teenagers are
unemployed. He further warned that if the economy does not improve in the near future, a whole generation of young blacks will

enter adulthood in the 1980s without ever having held a job. The implications and ramifications of such a situation are absolutely disastrous.[5] Already, an increasing number of black youths are dropping out of the labor force. As recently as mid 1979, 75 percent of black teenagers remained outside the workforce, compared with a rate of 50 percent for white youth. About a half of all black labor force dropouts are male teenagers.[6]

While such a situation may be disastrous to the black community, it serves the interest of the industrial order quite well. Afro-American youth now constitute the largest segment of the industrial reserve army. Capitalism maintains this category of workers at the lowest level of subsistence and uses them when its industries require additional workers in the event of economic expansion. At the same time they provide competition for other workers by seeking their jobs and, hence, depress wages in certain industries. Young black men are particularly appropriate for this role because they do not think of themselves as a class, they have few family responsibilities and possess little political consciousness or leverage. As the most powerless of a subjugated group, they are easily manipulated in this role.

One might dismiss the problem of the unemployment of black youths as being relatively insignificant in the overall picture of black oppression. Yet, to many low-income black families the additional income of their teenage children is vital to their existence. This is particularly true during a period when many adult males have lost their jobs. Moreover, many of these young blacks will themselves be heads of households. Almost one third of all black births in some inner cities are to black teenagers between the ages of 15-19.[7] When these teenage fathers are unable to find work, the children are forced into dependency on the meagre sum allotted to them by welfare institutions. Young black males face an economic reality entirely different from that of the white teenager, who can more effectively use his kinship and friend of the family network to secure employment.

An additional benefit to the economic order from the joblessness of black youth is their greater availability for the so-called "volunteer" army. As a result of the mass demonstrations against the war in Vietnam, the disaffection of middle class white youth for military service, the political state abandoned forced conscription into the armed services and decided to use volunteer personnel. Despite improvements in military pay and benefits, it attracted primarily those youth whose other options in life were less desirable than enlistment in the army. Thus, it was no surprise to see that in 1979 over 31 percent of the new recruits into the "volunteer" army were blacks. If there is any doubt about what class of black youth is "volunteering" for the army, it can be allayed by the figures which show that blacks make up 31 percent of the enlisted personnel (high school education or less) and only 7 percent of the officers' ranks (college education).[8] An obvious reason for black youths entering the armed forces in large numbers is their fear of entering the ranks of the underclass in the civilian world.

Many of them still find the military institution to be a mere extension of colonial society. In the army they have encountered a number of dehumanizing experiences such as racial slurs, the wearing of confederate flags by white soldiers, intimidation for wearing afro-style haircuts, assignment to more dangerous duty than whites, and failure to get assignments, medals and promotions on an equal basis with whites. White racism is unabated as black men leave the military scene. They receive proportionally more non-honorable discharges than whites in all branches of the service.[9] Yet, in 1973, 51.8 percent of all blacks eligible for reenlistment did so as compared with 32.5 percent of the eligible whites.[10] A major reason for this higher reenlistment rate is their knowledge that there are fewer job opportunities for them in the civilian society. For example, the unemployment rate for black veterans between the ages of 20–24 increased from 22.7 in the fall quarter of 1974 to 30.0 in the first quarter of 1975. Vietnam era veterans had an even higher unemployment rate — 50 percent.[11]

The proportion of blacks in the "volunteer" army declined in 1974 because of the spiraling jobless rate of whites who also flocked to its environs and the concern of the political elite about the implications of a predominantly black military force. There were probably just as many blacks who tried to enlist in the army but were denied entrance in favor of whites who made higher (or lower) scores on the Armed Forces Qualification Test.[12] While there may be a cultural bias in such tests, the lower score of blacks also reflects the substandard education they receive in the public schools. It is instructive to note that 66 percent of black enlistees have high school diplomas compared to 55 percent of white enlistees. Yet, it is in the area of education that young black men continue to suffer the fate of society's underclass.

THE COLONIAL EDUCATIONAL SYSTEM

Education for black youths has never been a high priority among the political rulers in the United States. Blacks continue to receive an inferior education at every level. And, it is partially this substandard education that maintains their colonial status. Moreover, within the educational institutions, the goals, values and attitudes of the white majority are the only ones that are accorded any legitimacy. The educational system selects those values and attitudes favored by Euro-Americans and conveys them to black youths as universal truths. School remains one of the major institutions for socializing young black men into the value system of the dominant society. In fact, the Afro-American youths are taught that the only legitimate social system is the same one that oppresses them.

Although whites marshal a violent fight against the desegregation of their schools, the benefits of school integration are also beginning to be questioned by many Afro-Americans. In many predominantly white schools, blacks find a kind of educational apartheid. Extensive use of a tracking system often consigns a majority of black students to the educationally slow classrooms. Even within the same classroom, the black student will discover that his white teacher expects little of him and subsequently he begins to expect little of himself. However, one group of researchers found that black students held positive images of their school performances when they were buttressed by their teachers. The results were still negative however, because the teachers were actually bestowing false praise on these black students in order to keep classrooms under control. Many of them were performing at a low academic level but thought they were doing well, a belief reinforced by their teachers. If white students were doing as poorly, they concluded, changes would most likely be instituted within the schools to improve their academic performance. But, white society expects Afro-American youth to do poorly and praises them all the more for it. [13]

Many of these black students will find it hard to secure employment in the labor force if they can not read well enough to fill out a job application form. A U.S. Office of Education study found that 23 million adults lack the competence to be effective consumers or wage earners because of deficiencies in reading, writing, computation and problem solving skills. And the weakest performances were found among black and Hispanic males. [14] But teachers find it expedient to give unrealistic grades and praise to those students so as to maintain order in the classroom. While discipline is obviously a large problem in America's schools, Afro-American youth are disproportionately punished for misbehavior. A study by the Children's Defense Fund revealed that black children caught fighting in the schoolroom are likely to be suspended while belligerent whites only get a lecture from the principal. [15]

It has generally been assumed that school integration would prove to be beneficial to black youths. But at least one researcher discovered some latent benefits for majority group control. For example, blacks in segregated schools are more politically aware and inclined to participate in politics than blacks in desegregated schools. Since political consciousness and participation had been more effective in achieving black gains than racially integrated schools, it would appear that racially segregated schools produced more positive results in terms of political understanding and behavior. [16] One result of the segregation of black students in their own schools has been the organization of a community of resistance against racial oppression. In classical Marxist terms, the concentration of a class of oppressed people in a central location tends to elevate their level of political consciousness.

Afro-American youths who become aware of the irrelevance of their education respond by dropping out or rebelling violently within the school. One survey reported 70,000 serious physical assaults on teachers each year and hundreds of thousands of assaults on students including more than 100 student homocides in 1973. [17] Those who drop out are increasingly joining the ranks of youth gangs. A common explanation for the growth of youth gangs is the lack of a father figure in the home and the consequent need to prove one's masculinity. But Johnson discovered that most of the black youth gangs in New York City were school dropouts who had begun to question the relevance of the educational process in changing the conditions they were destined to face. Many of the black youths in these delinquent groups had developed a distrust of the social order's authority figures.[18] They had become skeptical of the legitimacy of adult political authority. As Fanon has noted, the oppressed reject all visible representatives of colonial rule.[19]

Clearly, what is happening here is that many Afro-American youth are becoming alienated from the educational process, are dropping out of school and joining the ranks of the unemployed. While their rebellion against societal authority is politically correct, their behavior often involves anti-social acts against the black community. Most of the victims of black gang violence are other blacks. Their burglaries, muggings and rapes are mostly confined to the black community. Such a situation has made many black areas a place of fear for their residents. This is the segment of black youths who are clearly emerging as the lumpen prolitariat of our day. Marx saw them as a marginal, fringe group operating outside the moral boundaries of capitalist society. In colonial society, however, Fanon saw them as the main revolutionary force because they had nothing to lose.[20]

Black male youths are the main targets of domestic repression. They are the group most feared by white society. The figures on black male youths' unemployment curiously coincide with the percentage of that group "volunteering" for military service. On the educational front, black females have a higher level of education than black males in every category except doctorates. In 1977 the numbers of black women entering college from high school exceeded black males by 84,000.[21] Recently, there has been a decline in the proportion of black students entering college. A major reason is the decline of black male attendance. If these young black males are neither in college nor in the work force, we may likely find them among the criminals on the streets of black communitites.

CRIME AND VIOLENCE

It is in the area of crime and violence that black youths are clearly implicated. The largest numbers of crimes against the person and acts of theft are committed by black males under the age of 24. A majority of all homicide victims in the United States last year were black and the perpetuator of the crime typically was a young black male between the ages of 20 and 24.[22] Hence, it is of little surprise that the number one cause of death among black males aged 15 – 34 is homicide.[23] Between 1960 and 1973, the increase in homicide prevented any improvement in the life expectancy rate of black males. During that span of time, their life expectancy increased by only one-half year, compared to one year for white males.[24]

Furthermore, there is little doubt that the black males committing these crimes are members of the underclass. In 1972 black male inmates were 42 percent of the nation's jail population. Most of them were young, poorly educated, low-paid wage earners or unemployed prior to their arrest. About 59 percent of them reported an annual income of less than $3,000 a year. Some 51 percent were under the age of 24. Among those prisoners sentenced to death, 50 percent of them were black. Within that group of black death row prisoners, 35 percent of the blacks were under 24 years of age compared to only 9 percent of the whites.[25] It is in these types of figures that we see the tragic pattern of America's exploitative economy and its effect on black youth.

While America's chaotic and irrespor͵ible economy is the primary reason for the consignment of Afro-American youths to the ranks of the underclass and the prisons, there are other subtle influences in American life which socialize black youths into violence. Among them is the media. The emphasis upon violence in the mass media is undoubtedly related to acts of violence among black youths. It is estimated that by age 12 the average child has witnessed 10,000 acts of violence on television alone.[26] Since black children watch television more often than children from other groups, the impact of such violence is even greater. Although the number of "Blaxploitation" movies has declined in recent years, they fed black youths a steady diet of violence which far exceeded that in movies catering to white majority youths.

The black ghetto, moreover, is nothing more than a microcosm of colonial society. Violence is epidemic in the American social structure and it easily deserves its reputation as the most violent country in the world. Its homocide rate is twice as high as that of any other industrialized nation. While the victims of black violence are mostly other blacks, the white majority and its political leaders have set an example of violence for black youths, by their historical acts of aggression against Third World peoples in the United States and throughout the world.[27] As Fanon reminds us, it is the colonizer who introduces violence into the home and mind of the native. Colonialism is violence in its natural state.[28]

High rates of crime and violence among black youths are also a function of their oppressed status. Law enforcement patterns are partially responsible for racial differentials in juvenile delinquency rates. Many white policemen treat black youths differently because they dislike the belligerent behavior toward policemen. Lower class black youths living in high delinquency areas have a much higher risk of being discovered and adjucated as delinquents. The police officer who observes a middle class white youth committing an illegal act will send him home while the Afro-American youth is detained more often for the same crime. In one study it was reported that only 33.6 percent of the offenses committed by white juveniles were referred to the court while 64.8 percent of the black arrests were disposed of by court referral.[29]

Ghetto youths have some justification for their behavior toward policemen. Harassing black youths in white neighborhoods, breaking up groups of youths (not engaged in provocation) congregated on corners or in cars, the wanton shooting of young black males for petty crimes and arbitrarily searching them for weapons are acts calculated to produce negative attitudes. Young blacks learn early that the law symbolizes systematic and unpunished police brutality, judicial bias, governmental indifference and racial hypocrisy. The police represent the store and pawnshop owners, the landlords and other vested interests that live outside their community. At a very young age, black youths develop cynical attitudes toward politics and an illegitimate system as it relates to them. The police are the most visible symbol of an illegal system.

DEATH AT AN EARLY AGE

Throughout colonial America, Afro-American youths must struggle merely to survive. Their forms of coping with Euro-

American domination are often nothing more than a slow death for them. One of these coping mechanisms is simply to become so narcotized that their subjugation under colonial rule is tolerable. The use of heroin, for instance, is estimated to be as high as 36 percent among black males between the ages of 20–24 in some urban areas of the United States.[30] In New York City narcotic addiction is the greatest single reason for death of black youths, exceeding deaths from any other single cause.[31] While hard drug consumption has become pervasive throughout the United States, a disproportionate number of addicts still comes from the least educated and poorest segment of the black community.[32] Heroin use is purely and simply a way of coping with a society in which young blacks see themselves as powerless and without any kind of future.

The ramifications of drug addiction are quite serious for the black community. In order to purchase drugs of the hard variety, black youths have to drop out of school to spend full time supporting their habits. Most will have to engage in illegal activity to buy the drugs. A majority of the crimes committed in black communities are drug related. And, they are often the most abusive of crimes, resulting from the addicts' desperate need for money to support their habits. They steal from their parents, the infirm and elderly, young children and any other source that is accessible and vulnerable. However, one should not lose sight of the fact that drugs and narcotics are marketed for profit in this country and those who profit most from it live outside the black community.

Most of the victims of drug abuse will be young black men because they feel most keenly the despair and frustration of their lives under institutional racism. Even without drug addiction, death comes to blacks at an early age. Black youths are 50 percent more likely than white children to die before they reach the age of 20. But, even more important, is the fact that the biggest causes of deaths among white youths are accidents and cardiovascular diseases while it is homocides, suicides, drug abuse and accidents that account for deaths among black youths.[33] These racial differences in causes of death not only reflect the unequal life changes of black and white youths, but also are most poignant reminders of the tragic situation for black youths in this country. Since the youths are the future of a group, these differences are also an example of how institutional racism is breaking the back of the black liberation struggle.

The suicide rate and its characteristics reflect the subjective reality of many black youths. Among blacks in general the suicide rate is and has been lower than that of whites. A high suicide rate might be expected for members of the black population in the United States. In a society which admittedly is racist, blacks have been subjugated to a host of problems that create a constant state of rage and frustration in individual group members. However, the black suicide rate — with the exception of youths — has, historically, been lower than that of whites. A popular explanation for this unexpected racial differentiation in suicide rates has been the stronger social ties within the black community which sustains individual blacks in the face of adversity. The black church, particularly, has been a buffer institution which provided many blacks with an oulet for their frustrations in a society which penalized them daily for their racial membership.

In recent years there has been a pronounced increase in black suicide vis-a-vis white suicide. At one time the national black suicide rate was less than half that of whites (6.0 against 12.8 per 100,000 population per year). The latest available mortality data reveal a black suicide rate higher than it has been in half a century. In fact, among black males, aged 25–29, the suicide rate nationally is greater than that of their white age peers. Of course, in certain cities such as Washington, D.C., New York, and others, the suicide rate of black males under age 35 has long exceeded that of their white counterparts.[34] A significant racial difference in suicide patterns has been the tendency of blacks to reach their suicide peak in the early years, while this peak increases in direct relationship to advancing chronological age among whites.

Before examining the rates and causes of suicide among black male youths, it is necessary to note that this problem should be put into proper perspective. Self-destruction among blacks has definitely increased, but it still involves a small number of Afro-Americans. In 1975 suicide was the cause of death among 6.0 per 100,000 blacks. While this was a significant increase from the 3.0 per 100,000 population in 1965 it still ranked considerably below the death rates for hypertension, influenza or cirrhosis of the liver.[35] The peculiar nature of suicidal deaths tends to create a greater concern about their prevalence and each mortality from this cause creates a dramatic impact on the public consciousness.

Suicide is a particularly serious problem among black male youths. Death records since 1960 show that blacks aged 15–20 commit suicide at a rate higher than that of the total population of all ages.[36] The increase in black suicides has been highest in this group. Moreover, it is claimed by some behavioral scientists that if many of the black deaths that are labelled homicide were more seriously investigated, they would be revealed as suicides because the victim arranged or demanded to be killed.[37] At any rate, among black males in the age ramge 15–24, it is the third leading cause of death after accidents and homicides. It ranks number six among black females in the same age range.[38]

When we consider the causes of black youth suicide, the reasons will vary by sex and educational level. The basic demographic data on black suicide victims is very sparse and we must make generalizations on the basis of the limited evidence available. First, it appears that most suicides among young blacks occur among non-college students. This characteristic is related to the forces responsible for these suicides. While many whites commit suicide during their middle and later years because they did not achieve success according to their expectations, a large number of blacks kill themselves at very early ages because they believe there is no incentive for trying to achieve anything in a racist society. These low expectations are somewhat more common to black youth who have dropped out of high school and see little future for themselves in this country. With an unemployment rate as high as 65 percent among black teenagers, this is not a totally unrealistic perspective.

For the black college student or graduate, the cause of suicide may be related to the high expectations he has for success and the frustrations encountered in overcoming the persistent barriers against reaching his potential that result from racism. Although we have no data, it would not be surprising to find the suicide rate among black collegians to be much higher at predominantly white institutions than at black colleges. Within the white college the Afro-American student will have to cope with much of the same institutional racism he found in the outside world. Many a black student has been admitted to a white school under some special admissions program, only to find an irrelevant curriculum, racist and indifferent instructors and a totally incompatible social life. Whatever problems he encounters at a black college will not be as psychologically damaging as the forces present at a white college. Even in the most isolated environment, black colleges have a more conducive social atmosphere and provide a feeling of solidarity not found in most white universities.

Some black college students, of course, who commit suicide do so for reasons not directly related to institutional racism. A prominent suicidologist, Richard Seiden, notes that some students possess suicidal tendencies when they arrive on a college campus. Very often they are students who make good grades, but are somewhat passive and quiet with their fellow students. He cites one case where a student was so isolated from his peers that weeks passed before he was missed and was later discovered dead in his room.[39] The opposite case can also be found, particularly among black college students. Since many black college students come from homes where they are the first members of their family to attend an institution of higher education, they may feel more keenly the responsibility of doing well in school. If they find themselves performing at a low level, the inability to face failure may lead to their self-destruction.

Despite the stresses associated with being an Afro-American in college, the suicide rate is most likely higher among black youths, who do not attend college. However, the motives for black suicide have not been thoroughly investigated. Most research on black suicide has focused on the black male, and several reasons have been proposed to account for the phenomenon in this group. Among them is the theory that most black suicide is of the fatalistic type. Fatalistic suicide is a typology originally developed by the sociologist Emile Durkheim. It refers to the individual whose suicidal actions are a result of over-regulation by authority figures such as the police.[40] In such cases the individual feels that internal efforts are subordinate to external controls over his destiny. The situation of young black males is such that human effort, planning and volition cannot over come the impact that schools, employers, policemen and judges have on his life chances. Hence, crushed hope may lead to fatalistic suicide.

In a study of black male-suicides in New Orleans, a sociologist found that the majority of blacks who committed suicide had recently had difficulties with the police or law courts, while only 10 percent of the white suicide victims had such problems. Many of these black suicide victims had expressed fear of the police and a few had been quoted as having said they would kill themselves before going to jail.[41] The point to be emphasized here is that these black men saw the police as the operant enforcer and as the symbol of white authority over institutions in the black community.

What should be significant to the black community is that most black male suicide victims are killing themselves before the age of thirty-five. Just as many should be reaching the flower of their manhood, they find themselves locked in a life and death struggle with a massive and basically oppressive system of laws, customs, procedures and enforcers. In the words of James Baldwin, "To be a Negro in this country and to be relatively conscious is to be in a rage almost all the time."[42] To be black in this country, young, uneducated and unskilled is to be confined to the ranks of the unemployed, a permanent member of the American underclass. It means being unable to establish a home or family or to maintain either. The lack of family and occupational ties leads to further alienation and frustration. Such a situation, which is becoming more and more common, generates suicide because it creates a feeling of despair and apathy in the individual. And it is this sense of despair, the feeling that life will never be satisfying that blacks must face at a much younger age than whites.

SUMMARY

With the decline of America as an international power, and its escalating domestic problems, a natural solution is to have peoples of color bear the brunt of the fallout from what are problems resulting from the internal contradictions of monopoly capitalism. Confining problems of unemployment, poverty, and military conscription to that segment of the populace which is black and brown and powerless appeases the white majority prolitariat. When issues such as school busing, crime in the streets, and welfare are interpreted as matters of race, the races become polarized and less likely to unite on the basis of their mutual class interests. One might take note of the fact that the recent immigrants to America have come primarily from the Third World. And immigrants are traditionally given the lowest-paying and hardest jobs. All these factors illustrate the role of color in maintaining the consciousness of class at a low level in this country.

Within this political and economic context, young black men are destined to get the worst of both worlds. As the most dispensable members of the working class, their needs and problems will be given low priority by the elite. At the same time the existence of a youth culture gives rise to the theories of a generation gap. The rebellious, anti-authority behavior of youth is attributed to per-missive child rearing practices. Yet, this same rebellious behavior, when organized into a coherent social movement, helped fuel the civil rights and Black Power Movement, impede war in Indo-China, and fundamentally changed the character of the nation's colleges.

The two sides of youth's behavior exist simultaneously. Their challenge to traditional authority and practices is often very revolu-tionary in character. But, much of it is misdirected and apolitical in form. There is no inherent virtue in youth per se. Many black youths have become enmeshed in a web of machismo, which is manifested in narcotized and infantile behavior patterns which can isolate them from the adult black community. Yet, they contain the potential for revolution in their anti-tradition stance, and with the current attack on their very existence by the forces of institutional racism, they have nothing to lose.

Part II:
Crime and Violence

CHAPTER THREE:

Race, Masculinity and Crime

In the past hundred years criminologists have shown great interest in the relationship between race and crime. Various theories have been put forth to explain the association between racial membership and criminal activity. These theories have ranged from Lombroso's[1] discredited assertion that certain groups possess inherent criminal tendencies to the now widely accepted theory that certain racial groups are more commonly exposed to conditions of poverty which lead them to commit crimes with greater frequency.[2] The purpose of this chapter is to examine the relationship of race and crime in a theoretical framework which will permit a systematic analysis of racial crime within the political-economic context of American society.

The approach used here to explain race and crime is the colonial model. This framework has been formulated and used in the writings of Fanon, Blauner, Carmichael and Hamilton and Memmi and others.[3] It is particularly attributed to Fanon, whose analysis of colonial relationships in Africa has been used to explain the American pattern of racial dominance and subjugation. While there are many criminologists who will summarily dismiss this model as lacking any relevance for understanding the relationship between race and crime, it behooves us to give it a hearing since many blacks, especially those presently incarcerated, give it considerable credence. In fact, it is their definition of themselves as political prisoners that has motivated many prison protests in recent years.

Basically, the colonial analogy views the black community as an underdeveloped colony whose economics and politics are controlled by leaders of the racially dominant group. In this framework, it is useful to view race as a political and cultural identity rather than to apply any genetic definitions. Race is a political identity because it defines the way in which you are to be treated by the political state and the conditions of your oppression. It is cultural in the sense that white cultural values always have ascendency over black cultural values. Thus, what is "good" or "bad," "criminal" or "legitimate" behavior is always defined in terms favorable to the ruling class. The result is that black crime in America evolves according to the relationship of blacks to the colonial structure, in which racial inequality is perpetuated by the political state.

Obviously, there are some imperfections in the colonial analogy as a sole explanatory model to explain race and crime. We must have more theoretical and empirical research before mechanically applying the structural forms characteristic of classical colonialism to the complexities of crime in America. Yet, the essential features of colonialism are manifest in American society. Black men have been, and remain, a group subjected to economic exploitation and political control; they lack the ability to express their cultural values without incurring serious consequences. While other colonial factors such as the geographical relationship of the colonial masters to the colonized, the population-ratio, and the duration of colonization may be missing, they do not profoundly affect the form or substance of black and white relations in America which are based on white superordination and black subordination.

In using this model I am not discounting the complications of class often interjected into the issue of crime and race. However, domestic colonialism is as much cultural as economic. While members of the white working class are more victimized by their class location than other whites, they are not subjected to the dehumanized status of blacks of all social classes. The racist fabric of white America denies blacks a basic humanity, which permits the violation of their right to equal justice under the law. In America the right to justice is an inalienable right; but for blacks it is still a privilege to be granted at the caprice and goodwill of whites, who control the machinery of the legal system and the agents of social control.

The colonial model may also be used to explain the relationship between black masculinity and criminal behavior. When we speak of crime, it is automatically assumed that these are acts of men. Statistically, that is still the case. Although the incidence of criminal acts by women is on the rise, they still represent only four percent of the prisoners in the United States.[4] Under a system of internal colonialism, black men will be more likely to commit criminal acts or be arrested for such because the society denies them access to its goals. For example, women, at least those with children, may receive welfare assistance in order to support themselves. Failing that, they may turn to prostitution, a more lightly punished crime. Conversely, the colonized man must often turn to serious crime in order to satisfy the basic needs for food, clothing and shelter. Hence crime is, for some black men, a matter of sheer survival.

LAW AND ORDER

One of the key elements in securing the obedience of the citizenry to a nation's laws is their belief that the laws are fair. A prevalent view of the law among blacks is summed up in Lester's statement that "the American black man has never known law and order except as an instrument of oppression. The law has been written by white men, for the protection of white men and their property, to be enforced by white men against blacks in particular and poor folks in general."[5] Historically, a good case can be made for the argument that the function of law was to establish and regulate the colonial relationship of blacks and whites in the United States. Initially, the domestic colonial system was established by laws which legitimized the subordination of the black population.

The legalization of the colonial order is best seen in the Constitution itself. While the Constitution is regarded as the bulwark of human equality and freedom, it originally denied the right to vote to Afro-Americans and made the political franchise an exclusive right of white property owners. In fact, blacks were defined as a source of organic (or human) property for white slave holders in the notorious "3/5" clause. The clause allowed the slave owner to claim 3/5 constituency for each slave that he possessed. Since non-citizens are beyond the pale of legal equality, the Dred Scott decision in 1857 affirmed that slaves were not citizens and could not bring suit in the courts. The ultimate blow to black aspirations occured in 1896 when the Supreme Court upheld racial segregation in its "separate but equal" decision in the Plessy v. Ferguson case.[6]

In a contemporary sense, black men are not protected by American law because they have no power to influence those laws. They have no laws of their own and no defense against the laws of the colonizer. Thus, the power to define what constitutes a crime is in the hands of the dominant group and is another means of racial subordination. How crime is defined reflects the relationship of the colonized to the colonizer. The ruling caste defines those acts as crimes which fit its needs and purposes to be defined as such and characterizes as criminals those individuals who commit certain kinds of illegal acts, while other such acts are exempted from prosecution and escape public censure because they are not perceived as criminal or a threat to society.

As a result of the colonial administration's power to define the nature of criminality, white collar crimes which entail millions of dollars go unpunished or lightly punished, while those of the colonized involving nickels and dimes result in long jail sentences. The chief executive of the political state can wage a war that takes thousands of lives in direct violation of the Constitution, while the colonized are sent to gas chambers for non-fatal crimes such as rape. It is no coincidence that the two criminal acts for which politicians once wanted to preserve the death penalty were kidnapping and airline hijacking; the former a crime committed mainly against the wealthy, while the latter is most often a political crime against the state.

Crime is often seen as a racial issue in the United States because a majority of the violent crimes commited in urban areas involve black males. In particular, the type of crimes they commit such as robbery, burglary and assaults, are the ones which create the most public fear and concern. Yet, the greatest amount of money stolen is through white collar crime such as employee thefts, embezzlement, financial fraud, etc. Most white collar criminals are white males. It is estimated that white collar crime costs the nation as much as $200 billion dollars a year compared to $88 billion for street crime.[7] And, the greatest sources of violence in this country are unsafe automobiles and consumer products. Over thirty million Americans are injured and thirty thousand killed each year because of unsafe consumer products other than automobiles.[8] The call for law-and-order, however, is aimed mostly at the crimes of the poor and blacks. The findings of Bennett and Tuchfarber are instructive: the hardliners on law-and-order were Republican, middle class, white and elderly. Blacks, in spite of the fact that they were more likely to live in crime infested areas, preferred to identify and alleviate the conditions that breed crime and violence.[9]

AGENTS OF SOCIAL CONTROL

In any colonial situation, there must be agents to enforce the status quo. A classical colonial world is dichotomized into settlers and natives, and the policeman acts as the go-between. Fanon describes it in Colonial Africa:

In the colonies it is the policeman and the soldier who are the official in-stituted go-betweens, the spokesman of the settler and his rule of oppres-sion . . . by their immediate presence and their frequent and direct ac-tion, they maintain contact with the native and advise him by means of riflebutts and napalm not to budge. It is obvious here that the agents of government speak the language of pure force. The intermediary does not lighten the oppression, nor seek to hide the domination; he shows them up and puts them into practice with the clear conscience of an upholder of the peace, yet he is the bringer of violence into the home and into the mind of the native.[10]

One could hardly find a more perfect example of the role of the policeman than in the findings of the United States Commission on Civil Rights in the 1960s. Police brutality was discovered to be a fact of daily existence for Afro-Americans and a primary source of white abuse against any black challenge to the status quo. In essence:

Police misconduct often serves as the ultimate weapon for "keeping the Negro in his place," for it is quite clear that when all else fails, policemen in some communities can be trusted to prevent the Negro from entering a "desegregated" school or housing project, a voting booth, or even a court of law. They may do it merely by turning their backs on private lawless-ness, or by more direct involvement. Trumped up charges, dragnet roundups, illegal arrests, the "third degree" and brutal beatings are all part of the pattern of "white supremacy."[11]

Many white officers covet an assignment in the black community because it is financially lucrative. They find it easier to collect extortion money from petty ghetto criminals and are less likely to be detected, investigated or convicted since blacks believe it to be futile to report corrupt police officers. They also have a greater opportunity to receive outstanding merit citations based on the number of arrests they make or "crimes" that they solve. These awards allow them to achieve more rapid promotion, greater authority and higher salaries.

In order to enforce colonial rule, the policeman must have certain traits. First and foremost, he must be a member of the dominant racial group. Almost every major urban area has a police force that is predominantly white, although the cities themselves may be populated mostly by blacks. It is not only that the police force is composed mostly of members of the colonizer's group, but they also represent the more authoritarian and racist members of that sector. One survey disclosed that the majority of white police officers hold anti-black attitudes. In predominantly black precincts, over 75 percent of the white officers expressed highly prejudiced feelings towards blacks and only 1 percent showed sympathy toward the plight of blacks.[12] A series of public hearings on police brutality in Chicago revealed that candidates who do poorly on the psychological tests or who demonstrate personality problems while undergoing training in the police academy are assigned to "stress areas" in Chicago's black and brown ghettos.[13]

Considering the characteristics of policemen assigned to the black ghetto, it is no surprise to find that for the years 1920–1932, out of 479 blacks killed by white persons in the South, 54 percent were slain by white police officers.[14]. In more recent periods, according to a Police Foundation study, 75 percent of the civilians killed by police in seven cities between 1973–74 were black males. They concluded that many police shootings did not appear to have served any compelling purpose. They fell into a "middle ground" where it was difficult to determine if the shooting was justified or not. In nine out of ten cases, police who shot civilians were not punished.[15]

Even less surprising are the studies which indicate that blacks believe that policemen are disrespectful, that police brutality exists in their areas, and that blacks are treated worse than whites by the police.[16] These beliefs are based on two basic types of complaint besides the abuse suffered at the hands of the white police officer. One is that the police are more tolerant of illegal activities, such as drug addiction, prostitution, and street violence, that they would not permit in white communities. The other is that the police see as much less urgent the calls for help and complaints from black areas than from white areas.[17]

Distrust of white policemen is widespread in the black community. Even black police officers have expressed a distrust of them. A study of black policemen in Washington, D.C. revealed that a majority of them were not inclined to trust their fellow white officers.[18] In New York City about 3,000 black police officers quit the predominantly white policeman's association in protest over the union's support of a white officer accused of killing a black youth.[19] Further evidence of racism among white policeman comes from the former Sheriff of San Francisco, Richard Hongisto, who states, "I believe that I literally heard thousands of racially derogatory remarks cited by white police officers during the course of my ten years in the police department."[20] Almost every survey taken reveals that a larger number of blacks than whites hold unfavorable attitudes toward the police. Such a situation once led Louis Lomax to comment: "I don't know a single Negro who doesn't get a flutter in his stomach when approached by a white policeman."[21]

Such complaints about the police force stem from its functional role in colonial society. The police are not placed there to protect the indigenous inhabitants, but to protect the property of the colonizers who live outside that community and to restrain any black person from breaking out of the colonial wards in the event of violence. No amount of "proper" behavior on the part of the police, therefore, nullifies the fundamental colonial machinery which imposes law and order according to the definitions of the colonizer. The law itself constitutes the basis for colonial rule and the ideology of white supremacy shapes the police force, the courts, and the prisons as instruments of continued colonial subjugation.

CRIMES BY BLACK MEN

The colonial character of American society tends to structure the racial pattern of crime. In the urban areas where most blacks live, major crimes against property are committed by whites (68.3 percent white, 32.7 percent black). More blacks (47.9 percent) than whites (47.8 percent) are arrested for serious crimes of violence such as murder, rape, and aggravated assaults. These crimes of violence by blacks are most often committed against other blacks.[22] One survey reported that black males had a victimization rate of 85 per 1,000 population as compared with that of 75 per 1,000 for white males. It concluded that "the typical crime victim is black. He is a young black male — and a poor, uneducated black male at that."[23] The poorer a person is, the more likely it is that he or she will become a victim of crime.

The above statistics follow the typical pattern in the colonial world. The violence with which the supremacy of white values is affirmed, and the aggressiveness which has characterized the victory of these values over the lives and thoughts of the colonized man, means that his challenge to the colonial world will be to claim that same violence as a method of breaking into the colonizer's forbidden quarters. According to Fanon, colonized men will initially express this internalized aggressiveness against their own people. This is the period when the colonized terrorize each other, while the colonizer or policeman have the right to assault the colonized male with impunity. This pattern of intra-racial violence allows the colonized man to negate his powerlessness, to pretend that colonialism does not exist. Ultimately, this behavior Fanon states, should lead to armed resistance to colonialism.[24]

The cultural values of white supremacy place little premium on the lives of blacks in the United States. The death of a colonized man is of little importance to the continuation of colonial rule, except that it may deprive a particular colonizer of the labor of a skillful worker. Hence, while blacks are generally given longer prison terms than whites for the same crime, they get shorter sentences for murdering other blacks.[25] According to Bullock,

These judicial responses possibly represent indulgent and non-indulgent patterns that characterize local attitudes concerning property and intra-racial morals. Since the victims of most of the Negroes committed for . . . (murder) were also Negroes, local norms tolerate a less rigorous enforcement of the law; the disorder is mainly located within the Negro society. Local norms are less tolerant (in black crimes against white property), for the motivation to protect white property and to protect "white" society against disorder is stronger than the motivation to protect "Negro society."[26]

THE JUDICIAL MACHINERY

Colonial practices are not confined to the police. Rather, the political state (also dominated by whites) controls the dispensation of justice from police apprehension to prison, and these all serve the interests of the colonizer. Most judges in the State, Federal, Circuit, Superior and Supreme Courts are political appointees, not elected officials. No black person in this country has the power to appoint a judge to the bench. Consequently, we find almost no black judges in the South, and few in the North and West. A minority committee set up to advise the Justice Department noted that minorities comprise 50 percent of the nation's prison inmates but only 4 percent of its law enforcement personnel.[27] A study of courts in the South found that blacks hold only 6 percent of court jobs, although they comprise 20 percent of the area's population. Of the 112 Federal district judges in the region's 29 district courts, only one was black.[28]

A trial by jury does not guarantee equal justice to the accused black offender. Blacks are still systematically excluded from juries in some parts of the South and are often underrepresented on juries in which they are allowed to serve. Sometimes they are excluded by subtle and indirect means such as peremptory challenges by the prosecution; sometimes by more direct means such as requirements for voter registration, property ownership, or literacy tests. Despite the American creed of equal justice before the law, few black offenders before the courts will receive a neutral hearing before a jury of "normal" white Americans. In one study of hypothetical cases in which a plea of insanity was entered, whites tended to hand down more guilty verdicts for black males, although the basic information was the same for all groups.[29] As Fanon states, in a racist society the "normal" person is therefore racist.[30]

Blacks are further victimized by the lack of adequate legal representation. Since colonial administrations allow few natives to attain professional skills and become members of the native bourgeoisie, there is a scarcity of black lawyers to represent alleged black offenders before the courts. Another feature of colonialism is to make natives dependent upon members of the ruling group in order to achieve ordinary rights of citizenship. Thus, black defendents often choose white lawyers over black ones because they feel they can neutralize the impact of racism on decisions rendered by a white judge and jury. Many black defendents, of course, cannot afford an attorney and must accept a court-appointed lawyer. One investigation found that given identical circumstances and evidence in a murder trail, juries are twice as likely to convict a person defended by a black attorney as they are to convict if the legal counsel is white.[31]

Another disadvantage faced by black defendants is the illegitimacy attached to their cultural values by whites. There are several examples of words and phrases used by black men which have a totally different meaning in the white community. These cultural language differences are particularly crucial in certain types of crimes such as assault and battery and public obscenity. But, the colonial order insists that the native society is lacking in values, and that differences in cultural symbols, i.e., language, are not recognized in a court of law. There are other linguistic barriers in the courtroom that affect the black defendant. Often, he may not comprehend the legal jargon of the attorneys and gives answers based on his mistaken interpretation of the language used in the courtroom.[32]

Given all these factors, the black defendant is often short-changed in the decision of the court and the length of his prison sentence. They are particularly discriminated against when one considers their chances of receiving probation or a suspended sentence. For example, 74 percent of "guilty" blacks were imprisoned in state larceny cases compared to only 49 percent of guilty whites. The racial gap in larceny cases is greater than in assault convictions because black larcenies are more often committed against white men, while assaults occur more frequently against other blacks. Hence, racial disparities in prison sentencing are not only related to the skin color of the alleged offender, but of his victim, too.[33]

It is in the area of capital punishment that the racial, and thus colonial, factors stand out. The statistics on capital punishment in the United States reveal most glaringly the double standard of justice that exists there: one norm for the wealthy and another for blacks and poor people. Even the former warden of Sing Sing prison once remarked, "Only the poor, the friendless, and the foreign-born are sentenced to death and executed."[34] But, it is particularly the colonial wards of America, i.e., black males, who have suffered the most from this dual standard of American justice.

Since 1976, the Supreme Court has been considering capital punishment on a state-by-state basis, allowing it when local laws set clear guidelines as to when executions are justified. Some 37 states still retain the death penalty for certain crimes and there are still men on death row. One such state is Florida, where a black man is still more likely to receive the death penalty — if he murders a white person. In an analysis of first degree indictments for murder in Florida counties between 1972 and 1978, it was found that, overall, 17 percent of the black men who murdered whites were given the death penalty, compared to 3 percent whose victims were black. White defendants were more apt than blacks to win acquittal, be judged incompetent to stand trial or get their cases dismissed while blacks were much more likely to face trial and be found guilty. A bias against men was also evident as only 1.6 percent of female murder defendants drew the death penalty as opposed to 12 percent of the men.[35]

In another study covering three Southern states between 1973 and 1977, it was reported that only 6 percent of those arrested for homocide were blacks who killed whites but these blacks constituted 40 percent of the convicts on death row. Just 5 percent were blacks who killed other blacks. There has yet to be found a case where a white who killed a black has been placed on death row.[36] These results strongly suggest that the judicial system places a high value on white lives and a comparatively low value on black lives. Moreover, it is primarily the poor who are given the death penalty. Poor black male defendants typically have less than a high school education and are represented by public defenders.[37]

THE POLITICAL PRISONER

The combination of the colonial administration of justice and black oppression have coalesced to place a disproportionate number of blacks in the nation's prisons. The number of blacks in prison is 5½ times their representation in the society at large. The white detention rate is 159.8 per 100,000 as compared to the non-white rate of 888.4 per 100,000.[38] Yet, as Angela Davis has observed:

> Along with the army and the police, prisons are the most essential instruments of state power. The prospect of long prison terms is meant to preserve order; it is supposed to serve as a threat to anyone who dares disturb existing social relations, whether by failing to observe the sacred rules of property, or by consciously challenging the right of an unjust system of racism and domination to function smoothly.[39]

In recent years protests by black prisoners have been on the rise. Part of the reason is his definition of self as a political prisoner. We might define two basic types of political prisoners. One kind is the person arrested under the guise of criminal charges, because the state wishes to remove the political activist who is a threat to the prevailing racial conditions. Examples of these types were Angela Davis, Bobby Seale, H. Rap Brown, and the Wilmington Ten. The second type of prisoner is more numerous and consists of those blacks who are arbitrarily arrested and then railroaded through the courts where they face politically-appointed white judges, all-white juries and without a lawyer, or with a court-appointed lawyer who suggests a guilty plea in exchange for a reduced sentence.

According to official government statistics, one out of every four black men will go to prison at some time in his life. In some urban areas blacks and other minorities comprise as much as 90 percent of the prison population. If a man is poor, uneducated, a minority and is convicted of a crime, he stands a much greater chance of going to prison than his white counterpart. The link between imprisonment, poverty and race is clear. One study found a pronounced correlation between a state's unemployment rate and its crime rate. The higher the unemployment rate in the state the higher the incarceration rate. Moreover, the larger the black population in a given state, the higher the imprisonment rate of that state.[40] Loss of freedom is not the only consequence of imprisonment. Brutality and rape by prison guards are frequently reported by black prisoners. Punitive discipline is also unfairly used against black inmates as many have been placed in tiny single cells and kept in a "lock-down" situation for 23½ hours a day.[41]

One could not possibly take seriously the society's claim that prisons are designed to rehabilitate if one could observe their inner workings. In prisons where the majority of the inmates are blacks, Chicanos, and Puerto Ricans, most of the guards will be white, racist, and former policemen or soldiers. These prisoners will be subjected to the most dehumanizing conditions: urine is placed in their food; they are raped by prison guards, placed naked in solitary confinement without sanitary facilities, and tortured and murdered by prison authorities.[42] A common practice in prisons is the use of inmates for medical research. An Atlanta prison used prisoners to test a malaria serum in an experiment where the prisoners actually were infected with malaria, but treated before it could kill them. However, at least three prisoners suffered ruptured spleens from the disease and a few contacted hepatitis.[43] With such an abundance of horror stories, a number of authorities have called for the abolition of the nation's prison system.

Since most black crimes have black victims, not all black prisoners are, ipso facto, political prisoners. But, their incarceration stems from the subjugated condition of black people in the United States. As Chrisman asserts, "a black prisoner's crime may or may not have been a political action against the state, but the state's action against him is always political."[44] The basis for this judgment is that the black criminal is not tried and judged by the black community itself, but that his crime is defined, and he is convicted and sentenced by the machinery of the ruling colonial order whose interests are served by the systematic subjugation of all black people. As long as black crime occurs within the context of racial subjugation and exploitation, black men will continue to believe that their acts will not be objectively and fairly judged.

SUMMARY

In this chapter the colonial model has been used to explain the relationship between race, masculinity and crime. While the fit between theory and empirical data is not perfect, it does illustrate the link between black oppression and the disproportionate amount of crime found in the black community. The operational effects of colonialism are expressed in the high arrest rates, lengthy prison sentences, and political victimization of blacks in prison, and the path that leads to jail is deeply rooted in the imposed pattern of black subordination.

Crime, economic deprivation and masculinity are all intertwined. The prhase, "all men are equal before the law," may be occassionally true in the application of the law. However, as Balbus has noted, it is equally correct that legal equality in the face of the existence of economic inequality is repressive.[45] Even when a strong economic need is absent, black men may gravitate toward criminality in order to achieve cultural goals that are established for all members of the society. The masculine ethic of success leads them to commit illegal acts when the dominant culture restricts access to socially accepted ways of attaining those goals. Colonialism creates a feeling of alienation when the black male senses that he is not part of the society, that he is powerless to determine his life chances. In such a situation, the only law that is relevant to him is the law of survival.

Using the colonial model does point the way to reducing some of the inequities of American criminal justice. Among one of the remedies suggested by this model is community control of the police, which would diminish the black belief that the police in black neighborhoods constitute an army of occupation. An autonomous police force composed of members of the native group would eliminate the illegitimate use of violence against the black populace. Policemen would be controlled by the native community and required to live in their precinct. In this way blacks would have greater assurances that the police are present to respond to their interests and needs rather than to the needs of the white majority.

The judicial process needs to be reorganized along similar lines. Oppressed racial minorities should be allowed to have a trial by a jury of their peers. This means selection of a jury whose experiences and values are similar to those of the defendants. Where this is not feasible, proportional representation of blacks on juries, legal staffs, and judicial benches should be considered. While these suggestions will not radically affect the socioeconomic conditions that generate crime, they will at least reduce the impact of racism on the administration of justice to the black population.

Until such time as these changes take place, black crime will continue to exist at or beyond its present level. A major concern of the black community is the black-on-black crime in its environment. Some indigenous groups have organized to fight this type of crime in order to make their communities safe places to live. The colonial order has little concern for the safety of its natives and cannot be depended upon to solve their internal problems. Therefore, blacks must assume the responsibility for policing their own communities and simultaneously fight against the victimization of blacks by the criminal justice machinery of the colonial power structure.

CHAPTER FOUR:

The Masculine Way
of Violence

Some years ago the Civil Rights activist H. Rap Brown stated that violence is "as American as cherry pie."[1] The birth of the United States as a free nation was rooted in the violent overthrow of a dictatorial regime and this tradition of violence has permeated the social fabric of North America from that time to this day. By any statistical measure it outranks all countries in the world in the prevalence of violent acts. Its homicide rate is double that of all other industrialized nations. A number of its public officials have been victims of assassination or assassination attempts. Each hour of the day at least two Americans are homicide victims.[2] Such a pattern of violence led Sartre to label "that super-European monstrosity, North America, as a bastard child or satanic mutation of degraded Europe."[3]

Hence, black violence in the United States may be viewed as an exaggerated form of the normative pattern of violence in this cultural context. Although violent crime in this country is associated in the public mind with blacks, any review of history shows violence to be an institutionalized part of America's social structure. Beginning with the war against the Native American Indians, this country has rarely experienced a period without violent strife of some kind. Its wars alone have accounted for over four million American deaths, with even larger casualties for the enemy countries.[4] Labor strife, lynchings, riots, assassinations, mob violence are all part of this country's violent history.

The violent tradition in the United States is due partly to its frontier experience which cultivated a materialistic philosophy whereby sacred property rights superceded human rights, especially those of Native Americans and Chicanos.[5] Its contemporary cause may be found in the cultural supports for violence such as its anti-humanitarian values, prevalence of firearms, enshrinement of private property rights and a constant state of war-preparedness.[6] The latter is particularly important in creating a collective public predisposition toward violence. As Mills asserts, "war or a high state of war preparedness is felt to be the normal and seemingly permanent condition of the United States."[7]

In spite of its own combative history, this country is inordinately concerned and frightened over the violent acts committed by its men of color. While that is also the focus of this chapter, it should be noted that the incidence of violence in the United States is understood by the methods used to define it and by the methods used for law enforcement. Those acts of violence used in the interest of the political and economic elite are what might be called "legitimate" violence. Violence committed by members of America's underclass is regarded as illegitimate violence. Thus, the mass killings of workers, students or blacks by the police is seen as a necessary force. The murder of millions of non-combatants in a war is seen as necessary for national security. If we accept as a definition of violence any behavior designed to inflict physical injury on people,[8] it is clear that the greatest perpetrators of violence are American manufacturers. Each year over 30 million Americans are hurt and 30 thousand killed because of unsafe consumer products other than automobiles.[9]

It is because the people who run the government serve the interests of the manufacturers that laws are designed to punish only those who commit "illegitimate" acts of violence. For the most part they will be members of America's underclass, the poor and blacks. Therefore, it would be more accurate to see violence as a political act because its definition and the penalties for it reflect one's status in the society, not the objective fact of physical injury inflicted upon another person. The power to define and enforce laws against violence is contingent upon one's standing in a society stratified along class and racial lines.

VIOLENCE AGAINST BLACKS

Before examining the types of black male violence, it is necessary to note that in most instances of interracial violence, blacks have been the victims of white violence — not the reverse.[10] This has been true since the beginning of the slave trade, a practice itself which was responsible for the deaths of an estimated 100 million black people.[11] During the period of slavery, violence was normally used to intimidate and control the bondsman. There were no laws to protect a slave against the wrath of a white person. Except for his value as human capital, the slave could not escape acts of violence by any white person, and the free Afro-American was often the victim of white mob violence.[12]

After the end of slavery, blacks were still subjected to white violence. In the South it was frequently in the form of lynching. According to Wertham:

> Between 1882 and 1939 more than 5,000 Negroes were lynched in the United States, more than 1,800 since the year 1900. These statistics are incomplete, inasmuch as they do not include the countless and unaccounted persons who have been lynched in a clandestine way and just disappeared without getting into the statistics.[13]

Outside the South the most typical form of white violence against blacks was the white-dominated race riot. Between 1865 and 1940 over 500 blacks were killed in race riots and massacres.[14] It was rare to have white casualties in these disturbances since the violence originated with, and was controlled and directed by whites. In most cases the principal purpose was to inflict personal injury or death on Afro-Americans. Lynchings and race riots are examples of black powerlessness. These were occasions when the entire white adult population of certain communities in the United States collectively violated the law by attacking whole communities of blacks. The unilateral character of these riots led Myrdal to comment that "it was more a one-way terrorization than a two-way riot."[15] Yet, white law officials not only failed to enforce the laws which were violated but in some instances participated in the terrorism.

Collective white violence against blacks has declined in the last decade.[16] In turn black-on-black violence has increased along with the incidence of black violence against whites. It is the latter phenomenon that the law-and-order political campaigns exploit to gain white votes. But, the overwhelming majority of black acts of violence are directed at other blacks. It is the purpose of this chapter to examine those acts of intra-group antagonism and to analyze the forms of family and sexual violence, which dominate/terrorize/characterize black life today.

THEORIES OF BLACK MALE VIOLENCE

Various theories attempt to explain the reason for the high rate of black male violence. In an earlier period criminologists leaned toward a genetic explanation. Using a social Darwinist approach, Lombroso asserted that criminality was an atavistic throwback to an earlier evolutionary stage. Thus, "primitive" people (or those originally from "primitive" societies) possessed a predisposition toward criminal behavior.[17] This theory is largely discredited in most scientific circles today. The history of violence throughout the world reveals a pattern of the violent subjugation of non-white peoples by white settlers, therefore suggesting that centuries-old patterns of miscegenation and amalgamation tend to violate any assumption of racially defined groups as biologically unique.[18]

A more prominent theory is that of Wolfgang and Ferracuti, who believe that differences in attitudes towards the use of violence exist in specific populations and are organized into a set of culturally transmitted norms. Undergirding this theory is the assumption that lower class black males have a culturally transmitted value system which approves the use of violence for conflict resolution more so than is found in other American groups.[19]

Another theory of black violence is the regional tradition explanation of Pettigrew. He noted that Afro-Americans were primarily descendents of the Southern region of the United States and that this area has a markedly higher degree of violence than other parts of the country. This tradition of violence found in the South was, he asserted, responsible for the greater proclivity to commit homocide among blacks. Although the highest murder rates exist in large Northern cities, he thinks this can be explained by the large number of black migrants from the South in those locations.[20] In their migration to the North, Southern blacks carried values related to violence that they had learned as long ago as the era of slavery. Elkins has argued that the slave's only values were derived from the slavemaster. By identifying with the slave-holder's beatings, torture and rape of women, these values were internalized by Afro-Americans who bring a predilection toward violence with them to Northern states.[21]

Other theories of black violence are: (1) Violent acts are associated with relative deprivation. Rates of violence will be highest in areas where the occupational and income gap between blacks and whites is the greatest.[22] (2) Since means of masculine expression are often denied to Afro-American males, they rechannel these expressions into violent forms. A major reason for this need for violence to prove manhood is the lack of a male role model in the family. Uncertain of his masculinity, he adopts a tough, violent life most closely associated with the dominant culture's definition of maleness.[23]

Some of these theories are of questionable validity, others are deficient in failing to acknowledge the political economy of violence. The former is typical of the theories of black violence as deriving from regional mores and as a form of masculine expression. Violence in America is concentrated in Northern urban ghettos, not the South. Only three Southern cities are represented of the ten with the highest homocide rate and the majority of black violence in the North is not committed by Southern immigrants.[24] To contend that black violence in the North is a reflection of Southern ethos presumes a tenacity of the norms of violence which is transmitted intergenerationally.

The argument that violence is a form of masculine expression that black men need because of a deficit of male role models in their lives is limited as a unitary explanation. This theory is part and parcel of the matriarchy myth, which attempts to blame blacks for their own oppressed condition. Almost all black males have masculine role models, even if there is no legal husband or biological father within the nuclear family context. Men from broken homes dominate the violence statistics partly because fatherless black families represent the poorest of the poor, the most oppressed of the oppressed, and the men act out their frustration and anger. It is the relationship between racial oppression and black violence that should be examined.[25]

STRESS AND FAMILY VIOLENCE

The subject of violence in family relations has been neglected as an area of study by behavioral scientists until recent years. Most of the research has been carried out by criminologists and not by family sociologists. A primary reason for this void in the family literature on family violence has been the prevailing ideology of the family as a unit characterized by affection and cooperation between its members. Yet, it has been known for some time that the largest group of homicides in the United States involves spouses, kinsmen and close friends. In the Wolfgang study of homicide in Philadelphia during the period 1948–1952, over fifty percent of all homicides involved an altercation between family members and close friends. And one fourth of all homicides were family killings.[26]

It is difficult to discuss violence of any kind in America without noting the over-representation of blacks in the official statistics on violent crimes. In 1972 they were recorded as committing 60 percent of the homicides, 45 percent of the aggravated assaults, and 50 percent of the rapes in the United States.[27] Although there has been an increase in interracial acts of violence, the aggressor and victim in most acts of black violence are black. Most black violence is perpetrated against family and friends. It should be noted, however, that the proportion of homicides involving strangers is sharply on the increase.

Blacks are very prominent in those groups most likely to commit acts of family violence: the lower-class, large families, and the unhappily married. Hence, it is not surprising to find that romantic triangles or marital arguments add to the large number of violent crimes committed in the black community. One-fourth of all black homicides in 1972 took place among family members. A majority of them consisted of spouse killing spouse, and the others involved killings of a parent or child.[28]

While it may be simple to dismiss black violence as the result of that group's predisposition to it, the cross-cultural evidence does not support such an assumption. Bohannon's data from African societies illustrate that cultural, not biological factors, account for the high homicide rate among Afro-Americans. This is evident from his studies which show that African rates tend not only to be lower than Afro-American rates but also lower than rates for the general American population.[29]

While I do not uncritically accept the theory of Frantz Fanon about the therapeutic effects of violence among oppressed peoples, he does provide a guideline for understanding black violence in his supposition that the colonized man will initially be violent against his own people and that the development of violence among the oppressed colonial subjects will be proportionate to the violence exercised by the colonial regime.[30] Thus, it is understandable that the victims of black violence are primarily other blacks and that the white majority and its government leaders have set an example of violence by its historical acts of aggression against Third World peoples in the United States and throughout the world.

SOCIALIZATION INTO VIOLENCE

Lower-income black children are exposed to violence at very early ages. In housing projects, for instance, it is not at all uncommon for young children to have been shot at, robbed and raped by the time they reach the age of ten. The structure of low-income public housing projects is conducive to certain forms of crime such as rapes on the stairwell, robberies in elevators and sniper shooting from windows. Hence, children living in these areas that are relatively unprotected by the police, must learn to protect themselves.[31] Other forms of resolving conflicts are subordinated to physical skills which will prevent one from being overwhelmed by those who will test a person's toughness.

The status-conferral system in black life initiates the youth into acts of aggression. In the ghetto, the highest level of esteem and respect is reserved for the best streetfighter in the neighborhood. Older males in this environment encourage children to develop aggressive tendencies by their philosophy that a "real" man is supposed to fight. In altercations, older men can often be observed encouraging youths to fight. Claude Brown comments that in Harlem the people everyone respected were the men who had killed somebody. And, the children respected by the adults in their neighborhood were those who did not let anybody beat them.[32]

The black ghetto, however, is nothing but a microcosm of the entire society. Violence is endemic to the American social structure and America easily deserves its reputation as the most violent country in the world, while public officials decry violence by oppressed minorities. The public support for former President Carter's invasion of Iran to free American hostages is but one example of the cultural supports for violence in this country. Americans are the most heavily armed citizenry in the world.[33]

SEXUAL AGGRESSION

Sexual attacks against women are pervasive and sharply increasing in this country. The typical rapist is a black male and his victim is most often a black female. However, the most severe penalties for rape are reserved for black males accused of raping white women. Although 50 percent of those convicted for rape in the South were white males, over 90 percent of those executed for this crime in that region were black. Most of their alleged victims were white. No white male has ever been executed for raping a black woman.[34]

One of the most salient aspects of internal colonialism is the status of women and the question of sexual access. Historically, the white male has had both black and white women available to him. This is one of the privileges of white males in a racist society, and it contributes to the domination of black men. While white women have been unavailable to black men, there was no such protection for black women who were subjected to habitual abuse and sexual prostitution by white males.[35] The rape of black women by white men, has, historically, not been a punishable offense in American common law or by community standards. Most cases of interracial rape reported today involve black men and white women.[36] As has been noted, "no black woman would report being raped by a white man to the police in Oakland. They might report it to the Panthers but never the police."[37]

The prohibition of unions between black men and white women is an important aspect of majority rule. Myrdal is in agreement with this idea when he states: "what whites ask for is a general order according to which all Negroes are placed under all white people and excluded from not only the white man's society but also from the ordinary symbols of respect. No Negro shall ever aspire to them, and no white shall be allowed to offer them."[38]

Regardless of white society's taboo on black aspirations to white privileges, it is precisely the wish of the black male to take the Euro-American male's place. At least, it is Fanon's contention that the African male is an envious man who covets all the European's possessions; to sit at his table, to sleep in his bed and to sleep with his wife.[39] The rape of white women by Afro-American men often reflects this desire of the African. Cleaver thus explains his past history of crime:

> Rape was an insurrectionary act. It delighted me that I was defying and trampling upon the white man's law, upon his system of values, and that I was defiling his women — and this point, I believe was the most satisfying to me because I was very resentful over the historical fact of how the white man had used the black woman. I felt I was getting revenge.[40]

And, it was due to this fear of the black male invading his domain, destroying his property, that the settler punished severely any black man who attempted to become familiar or intimate with the symbol of white privilege — the white female. Many of the lynchings in the South were brutal reminders to black men that intermingling with white women was regarded as an unmentionable crime.[41] In recent years the function of lynch mobs has been transferred to the political state. From 1930 to 1964, 89 percent of the 455 men officially executed for rape in the United States were black. Bowers reports that 85 percent of all executions for rape have involved black men and white victims.[42]

However most contemporary rape cases are intra-racial. Despite white fear of the omnipresent black rapist, only ten percent of all rape cases involve a black male and white woman. In fact, it is the black woman who should be wary of rape since her chance of being assaulted is much higher than that of a white woman.[43] The protection that is denied black women from white male sexual attack often is not provided from black men either. Hammond found that what is often considered as strong-arm methods or even "rape" in the middle class terms was often quite a commonplace practice in the housing projects in Saint Louis.[44]

As is probably true of white females, the incidence of rape of black women is underreported. Ladner reported that an eight year-old girl has a good chance of being exposed to rape and violence if she is a member of the black underclass.[45] The examples of black males who have "taken it" from black women are probably known to us all. Widespread incidents of this kind are rooted in the sexist socialization of all men in this society. It is pronounced among black men who have other symbols of manhood blocked to them. Various explanations have been put forth to explain why black men rape their women. Poussaint attributes it to the tendency of black men to adopt the attitudes of the majority group toward black women. Because white men have historically raped black women with impunity, many black males believe they can do the same.[46] That they are often correct in that assumption is depicted in the saying of Sapphire that she realizes that "it is useless to report being raped because no one will believe that she didn't just give it away."[47]

Sexual violence is also rooted in the dynamics of the black dating game. The majority of black rape victims are familiar with their attacker, who was a friend, relative, or neighbor. Many of the rapes occur after a date and are what Amir describes as misfired attempts at seduction.[48] A typical pattern is for the black male to seek sexual compliance from his date, encounter resistance which he thinks is feigned, and proceed forcibly to extract sexual gratification from her. Large numbers of black men believe sexual relations to be their "right" after a certain amount of dating. A truly reluctant black woman is often victimized by the tendency of some black women to play a coquettish role in resisting male sexual demands, when they actually are willing to engage in sexual intercourse. Such a pattern of assault is defined as situational and led feminist Germaine Greer to label seduction as a four letter word — rape.[49]

Rape, however, is not regarded as the act of a sexually starved male but rather as an aggressive act toward females. Students of the subject suggest that it is a long-delayed reaction against authority and powerlessness. In the case of black men, it is asserted that they grow up feeling emasculated and powerless before reaching manhood. They often encounter women as authority figures and teachers or as the head of their households. These men consequently act out their feeling of powerlessness against black women in the form of sexual aggression.[50] While such a characterization of black rapists may be fairly accurate, rape should be viewed as both a sexual and political act because it is an externalization of social repression, such as racial prejudice, which is a barrier to normal expression of manhood for black males.

Manhood in American society is closely tied to the acquisition of wealth. Wealth is power — power to control others. Men of wealth rarely rape women because they gain sexual access through other means. The secretary or other female exployee who submits to the sexual demands of a male employer, in order to advance in her job, is as much an unwilling partner in this situation as is the rape victim. The rewards for her sexual compliance are normatively sanctioned, whereas the rapist does not often have the resources to induce such sexual compliance. Moreover, it is the concept of women as sexual property that is at the root of rape as a crime that is, *ipso facto*, a male transgression. This concept is peculiar to capitalistic, European societies rather than African nations where the incidence of rape is much lower. For black men, rape is often an act of aggression against women because the kinds of status men can acquire through success in a job is not available to them. This act of aggression affords a moment of power, and, by extension, status.

MARITAL CONFLICT

Homicides and assaults committed by spouses are rather pervasive in lower class black communities. At one time the murder of a spouse constituted one-fourth of all the homicides committed in this country. It is primarily a crime of the lower class as reported in official crime statistics. While domestic quarrels occur quite often among middle and upper class couples, they do not report them with the same frequency as the poor. Despite the underreporting of spousal violence by the upper classes, it is probably still more common among lower class blacks for reasons associated with their socio-economic and racial status. Strauss and his associates found the rate of wife abuse to be higher among blacks than in any other racial group, and that wife abuse was nearly 400 percent more common in black families than in white families.[51] When Cazanave and Strauss established a control group to study income, it was revealed that family violence occurred less frequently in middle-income black families than in middle-income white families.[52]

Contributing to spousal violence in lower class black families is the normative expectation that some physical violence against the wife is natural or necessary. In Chicago, for instance, a good "old man" is defined as one who "may slap or curse his old woman if he's angry but definitely not beat on her all the time when he's sober or endanger her life when drunk."[53] The husband is expected to use his physical superiority over his wife on occasions and frequent reference is made by lower class black men to the belief that they are supposed to treat women roughly to keep them in line. The study by Cazanave and Straus revealed that black respondents reported more approval of spouse slapping than white resondents. Black husbands were also three times as likely as white husbands to have slapped their wives and engaged in severe violence within a given year.[54] A major class difference, without regard to race, is that physical domination by a spouse is seen as an intolerable behavior pattern by many middle class wives. The first blow struck by a husband is taken by some of them as a symbol of gross abuse and it alone can result in divorce action.

Among the reasons for violent marital conflict are disputes over money, jealousy or drunken behavior. Jealousy is most likely the primary cause of spousal violence. Because of a community norm that encourages extramarital affairs, a liaison with another man or woman may ensue in a violent conflict between spouses.[55] Black families may be particularly subject to this stress in a marriage because of the belief by black husbands that a wife will seek sexual gratification elsewhere if relations do not go well. Such a belief may not be without foundation since one study revealed that one-half of their black female subjects condoned extramarital relations for the wife under certain conditions.[56] Men who are only living with, but not married to, a woman are even more prone to violence motivated by jealousy. One man commented that, "I figure if you are just staying with a woman and you're not married to her, she's as much somebody else's as she is yours." Sometimes, being married to a woman is regarded as a license for physical domination of her. According to this man, "If that's your wife, can't nobody say nothing. If you want to whip her, you can whip her."[57]

An unusual characteristic of black spousal violence is the incidence of black female aggression. In African societies, men are almost always the aggressor in domestic homicides.[58] But the American black women "has a reputation for using razor blades and lye to take care of business when he pushes her too far."[59] Boudouris in his analysis of homicides among family relations in Detroit during the period 1926–1968, found black women were the defendant in 44 percent of the court cases.[60] According to Cazanave and Straus, black wives were twice as likely to have engaged in serious violence against their husbands as white wives.[61]

Upon further investigation of these family homicides, it appears that the high rates of murder for black women can be explained as acts of self-preservation when attacked by their spouses. Such an explanation is borne out by the findings of Wolfgang that one-third of the homicides he analyzed showed that it was the victim who committed the first aggressive act.[62] However, it can also reflect the low status of black men in their family relations because of their inability to find jobs or because they are employed at jobs which pay very low wages.

The class characteristics of individuals involved in violent marital conflict are a natural result of their racial status. High rates of unemployment and underemployment automatically consign the majority of blacks to the underclass and several factors influence the incidence of marital violence. In the higher social classes, both black and white, men are able to exercise control over their wives in other than violent ways. Middle class men have more prestige, money and power than lower class men. Hence, they possess greater resources with which to achieve their aims with intimates.[63] The balance of power in marriage belongs to the partner bringing the most resources to the marriage. In general, money has been the source of power that sustains male dominance in the family. As has been noted elsewhere, "money belongs to him who earns it, not her who spends it, since he who earns it may withhold it."[64]

Lower class black males often find themselves at a disadvantage vis-a-vis their wives within the family. As a result of their consignment to the underclass, they are often unable to provide for their families properly and have a problem maintaining status in the eyes of their wives and children. Because they are aware of their role failure, they are inclined to counter-attack any perceived challenge to their manhood with violence. Rainwater observed that beatings and arguments precipitated by a husband seem to occur particularly when there is a discrepancy between the demands on him as a provider and his ability to meet those demands.[65] Hence, he responds violently in an attempt to regain status and respect for his role as head of the family.

The incidence of domestic violence is probably higher among lower class blacks than poor whites. A major reason for this intra-class difference is due to the strictures of racism. It is the internal devaluation of their self-worth as individuals that precipitates much of black violence. Comer reports that violent behavior against other blacks is often a displacement of anger toward whites. Since many blacks have little power to affect change, overwhelming obstacles and hopeless surrender produce high levels of frustration.[66] In the words of psychiatrist Alvin Poussaint, "Frustrated men may beat their wives in order to feel manly. These violent acts are an outlet for a desperate struggling against feelings of inferiority."[67] It has only been in recent times that this rage and anger has been turned against whites.

Marital violence among blacks is primarily related to the poverty, oppression and cultural values found in a racially stratified society. Blacks are not predisposed toward violence any more than other groups. But, in a society which dehumanizes them, as well as economically exploits them, psychological controls are broken and violent rage against the safest and most accessible person ensues. Environmental factors place such stress on blacks so as to make the incidence of marital violence much higher than among the white majority population.

PARENT-CHILD VIOLENCE

Parental abuse of children is nothing new. In earlier periods it was believed that children were inherently sinful and this evil must be violently exorcised. Among Americans of African descent, however, children have historically avoided much of the abuse heaped upon their white counterparts. The love of the African and Afro-American mother for her children is strongly documented in the historical records.[68] However, in recent years an increasing trend in parental injury to children has been evident among blacks. In fact, in the years 1967–68, the child abuse reported for black children was 21.0 per 100,000 in comparison to 6.7 per 100,000 white children.[69] Much of the racial difference in the statistics can be attributed to reporting bias but it also reflects the effect of environmental stress on black parent-child relationships.

Among the factors responsible for black child abuse are the conditions of poverty under which many children are reared. Child abuse is primarily concentrated in the lower class. These families, especially if they are black, are much larger than middle class families. Black families with four and more children were twice as likely to have a reported case of child abuse than similar families.[70] Moreover, those families have less living space in which to rear their children than more affluent families. Many of them are headed by a woman, who must often work outside the home and take care of her children afterwards. Such a difficult set of factors frequently leads to abusive behavior toward children.

The child-rearing methods of low-income parents are cited as an important cause of child abuse. While middle class parents tend to use verbal reasoning and psychological techniques with their children, lower class parents often use physical punishment to exact child obedience. As was true of their parents, most lower class parents believe that the way to make a child learn is to beat him. While alternate forms of punishment may also be used, a beating is eventually employed to force the child to conform to parental instructions.[71] However, some authorities believe that middle class child rearing techniques can be just as violent (although only verbal) and as psychologically damaging to children as those in the lower class.[72]

Many of the studies that deal with the discipline of the black child are limited. They typically measure attitudes toward the use of corporal punishment, but do not assess actual incidents. The findings of Cazanave and Straus indicate most black and white parents are very similar in their frequency of their approval of slapping or spanking a 12-year-old. They discovered however, that blacks were less likely to report actually having done so within a given year. Black and white families also reported very similar rates of severe violence against children. One reason, they say, that blacks practice less child abuse than expected on the basis of their low income, high unemployment and rejection by the rest of the society, appears to be the aid and support, particularly in the care of children, provided by black extended families.[73]

At any rate, the physical method of child behavior control can and does lead to excessive injuries to some children. But, in exacting child obedience, many lower class parents are without other effective means of accomplishing this objective. They cannot offer the more significant status rewards to their children. They are unable to reward their children for good behavior because they lack the educational and social privileges of the middle class.[74] Very few of these resources are available to black children in the underclass.

The conventional wisdom is that women are the main offenders in child abuse. But, abuse by men is often far more frequent and severe, considering the amount of time they spend with the children. During periods of layoffs and economic recession, fathers are increasingly put in contact with their children for many more hours a day and some are driven to hurt them physically. Increased unemployment is definitely correlated with incidences of child abuse as socio-economic circumstances lead to heightened stress in the family's life. The Cazanave and and Straus study found economic factors to be paramount in the causes of child abuse. Their data revealed a child abuse rate in families where the husband is a manual worker which is 41 percent higher than in families where the father is a white collar worker. Among husbands who are dissatisfied with their standard of living, the child abuse rate was 61 percent greater than the rate for other husbands.[75]

While most people conceive of parent-child violence as commonly involving the parent as the aggressor, there are a number of incidents in which the parent is the victim. An increasing number of violent acts, including homicide, are committed by youth under the age of 15.[76] The lack of status and economic resources among lower class black families means that many parents are unable to control a child's aggressive behavior toward them. An enormously high unemployment rate among black teenagers in the inner cities is also a contributing factor.[77] Being a poor, uneducated young black male in an oppressive environment without any means of escape, and having observed violence throughout his childhood, are explosive forces which erupt in aggression against those who are physically accessible, namely the parents.

SUMMARY

In this chapter I hve tried to show how acts of black male violence and environmental stress factors are inextricably linked. While other forces operate in the incidence of family conflict that may transcend race, the crucial variable in intra-family violence among blacks has been their status as a devalued racial group. There is no reason to believe that the lower class black male is any more prone to violence than males in the middle class or general white population. Yet, they are so over-represented in the official statistics on crimes of family violence as to preclude any explanation other than that racial and economic forces are responsible for the amount of violence in their family constellation.

While the most pronounced trend currently is the increase in stranger assaults and homicides, this does not necessarily reflect a decrease in the number of intra-family acts of violence. With the attendant fragility of marriages, female-headed households and parent-child tensions, violence continues to be a primary source of conflict resolution in the family. It is a pattern of violence that was introduced to Afro-Americans during slavery and has persisted throughout their existence in this country. While a greater emphasis on family solidarity, respect for women, and value of children can do much to reduce the amount of violence within the black family, only by eliminating the cause of, and cultural support for, violence in the larger society can we expect to live free from danger in an environment that is safe and free from harm.

Part III:
Sex and Sexuality

CHAPTER FIVE

The Myth of Black Sexual Superiority: A Re-Examination

Some years ago this writer raised the question: Are blacks sexually superior? My answer at that time was "if sexual superiority means to enjoy the pleasures of sexual congress without feelings of guilt and fear, and to be freed from the restraints of white puritanism, then the answer must be affirmative."[1] In the intervening period, there has been a dramatic increase in the frequency with which most white Americans engage in various sexual activities and in the number of persons who include formerly rare or forbidden techniques in their sexual repertoires.[2] These changes have given rise to the need to re-examine the question of black sexual superiority in light of what is regarded as the white sexual revolution.

A review of the past record of white beliefs about black sexuality casts in bold relief the view that "for the majority of white men, the Negro represents the sexual instinct (in its raw state)."[3] As long ago as the 16th century Englishmen imputed to Africans an unrestrained lustfulness and described them as "large propagators and hot constitution'd ladies." Certainly, in comparison to the dictums of Europeans about chastity being the best state for men and their norms that women should not enjoy sex under any circumstances, they contended that Africans represented the sexuality of beasts and the bestiality of sex.[4] History, however, tells us that Europeans were not always a puritanical culture.[5] Some claim that the beginning of human society (i.e. white society) was characterized by unrestrained sexual relations between man and woman, father and daughter, mother and son. Only with the development of private property, when men needed proof of paternity in order to will their resources to the right heir, were rules describing sexual exclusivity for women only brought into existence and mostly among the propertied classes.[6]

On the African continent, at least South of the Sahara, the view, in general, of sex was directed toward both physiological and psychological adjustment. Tribal values governing sexual behavior were strongly woven into the social structure and the first instinctive manifestations of sexuality were conditioned by traditional mores and environment. Public rituals often existed to confirm the appropriate sexual elements and to remove the improper ones. Whereas Europeans saw sex as inherently sinful, the African norm was that breaches of tribal sexual law were offenses against individuals and social groups, not against God. The African was concerned with crime and not with Sin. Conversely, it is impossible to generalize about sexual mores since there were large numbers of Africans who imposed harsh penalties on women who did not enter the conjugal state as virgins as well as many who allowed youths to satisfy sexual desires before marriage.[7]

It was with these diverse sexual values that Africans were brought to this country as slaves. There is sufficient evidence in the slave narratives, the slaveholders' own records and in the considerably lighter hue of some Afro-Americans, that those tribal norms were contravened on a massive scale, whenever possible and by bondsmen, overseers and slavemasters alike. However, within the slave quarters there were boundaries imposed on sexual activities among the inhabitants. A relationship between one man and a woman was respected and whenever possible they confined their sexual relationships to each other.[8]

It was during slavery that attempts to emasculate the black male were made, motivated by the fear of his sexual power. As Bernard has stated, "the white world's insistence on keeping Negro men walled up in the 'concentration camp' was motivated in large part by its fear of their sexuality."[9] One needs a deep understanding of the importance of sex in the United States in order to see the interrelationship of sex and racism in American society. In a society where white sexuality has been repressed, the imagined sexual power of the black male poses a serious threat. According to Hernton:

There is in the psyche of the racist an inordinate disposition for sexual atrocity. He sees in the Negro the essence of his own sexuality, that is, those qualities that he wishes but fears he does not possess. Symbolically, the Negro at once affirms and negates the white man's sense of sexual security. . . . Contrary to what is claimed, it is not the white woman who is dear to the racist. It is not even the black woman toward whom his real sexual rage is directed. It is the black man who is sacred to the racist. And this is why he must castrate him.[10]

After slavery ended Afro-Americans probably did have a more permissive sexual code than many Euro-Americans, but that fact has to be placed in the proper historical context. In accordance with Freudian theory, we can assume that the sexual drive exists in all individuals and has to be expressed in some form.[11] Historically, males in this culture have been allowed unrestrained libidinal expression. It is women on whom the greatest restraints have been placed, especially bourgeois women. Among working class white women the norm of chastity has been honored more in the breach than in its observance. A major reason for the class difference is the greater use of economic resources by bourgeois males to exact sexual chastity from the women in this class. Where there is no exchange value of sex for material reward, the libido thrives in a more liberated way.[12]

Thus, because the black masses enjoyed a more healthy sexual equality than was possible for whites in the post bellum era, a more permissive sexual code developed. Moreover, some of the controls on Euro-American sexuality did not exist in the same degree among Afro-Americans. The puritanical exhortations of organized religion served to effectively check much of the Euro-American's sexuality, while the black church functioned more as a tension-reducing institution and eschewed monitoring the moral standards of its parishioners. Black males did not classify women into bad and good groups on the basis of their virginal status. White men did make these distinctions and women were eligible for the respectability of marriage according to their classification in one group or the other. During an epoch in which the majority of white women were economically dependent on their men, this classification was an effective censor of female sexuality. Black women, in the main, were more economically and psychologically independent.[13]

Another reason the black church failed to censor the morals of their members was the image the black minister maintained as a sexual man. Because of his high status in the black community it was natural that many women would find sexual appeal in his prestigious status, his command of oratory, his wealth and flamboyance. However, the normative role of a minister is distinctly non-sexual. When warning his members against succumbing to temptations of the flesh, he is expected to be a perfect example by his display of sexual abstinence. Yet, as Hernton comments, the common songs, myths, jokes and ditties about the sexual activity of the black preacher are legend. It is asserted that not only have black women historically been sexually attracted to their preacher but also that black men too have identified with his unrestrained sexuality. This image of the black preacher is regarded by some as the last survival of African sexual heritage in black America, since he represents the legendary phallic symbol that was commonly worshipped in some African societies.[14]

THE CLASS FACTOR

One sees the operant effect of class as a differentiator of sexual expression by looking at variations in the black community itself. While the black bourgeoisie, until recently, has represented only a small segment of the total black community, its sexual values and behavior were often a reflection of the white bourgeoisie. Fairly conservative sexual attitudes were typical of middle class blacks as were premarital chastity and female frigidity. Many bourgeois Afro-American males preferred that their wives stay at home rather than work. Frazier once observed that "there is much irregularity in this class. The importance of sex to this class is indicated by their extreme sensitivity to any charge that Negroes are more free or more easy in their sexual behavior than whites."[15] In its most extreme manifestation, their sexual conservatism was reflected in the *in-loco-parentis* position of black colleges. In the 1920 s Fisk University had printed regulations that "it was forbidden for two students of the opposite sex to meet each other without the presence and permission of the Dean of Women or of a teacher." A girl and boy could be sent home for walking together in broad daylight.[16]

This is not to say that there are no moral parameters among the black working class or that all of their sexual values and behavior are healthy. In particular, we have to re-examine the stereotype of black sexual superiority as it relates to fulfilling the needs of both men *and* women. Furthermore, sexual competency must be defined as more than the physical fusion of bodies and consummation of the act of intercourse. We must also consider the psychological properties of the sex act, its misuse by both participants and how open blacks are to its total dimension, as well as to alternative sexual life styles. In part, this re-examination is forced by the new realities facing the black community and through increasing awareness that any sexual act that is biologically possible may have a socially redeeming value.

SEXUAL SOCIALIZATION

No matter how positive the eventual outcome of black working class sexual socialization, the process by which this class acquires its sexual values leaves much to be desired. From the limited data on the subject, it is apparent that black parents are not the source of sex education for most black youths. The majority of them, in fact, receive their initial knowledge of sex from peers and other sources. And, much of that information is fragmented and inaccurate.[17] While it is often assumed that blacks are much earlier exposed to sex than whites, the Kinsey group found that whites tend to learn about menstruation, fertilization, pregnancy, abortion, and prophylactics at slightly younger ages than blacks. Furthermore, white males experienced their first ejaculation from any source earlier than black males and the black women reported experiencing less nudity in their childhood homes than their white counterparts.[18]

More important than the age at which they acquire their sexual education is what many young black men learn. To wit, sex is considered a well formulated system for manipulating and controlling women. Early in the life cycle young men realize that money and women are the two most highly valued objects that they can gain in this system. As Hammond reports, women can supply a man with money or what it can buy, and they can be a means of satisfying his sexual desires. Hence, a competitive system emerges among men to make as many sexual conquests as possible. It is a dog-eat-dog system whereby the man with the best rap, flashiest clothes or coolest style wins — with women as the spoils.[19] Lost in this struggle for one-upsmanship is a feeling of relatedness toward women and an articulated awareness of their human qualities.

A most blatant indicator of the woman qua property ideology among many black men is the violence that often accompanies the sexual conquest. Witness, for instance, the common and legendary practice of "taking pussy." The strongarming of black women into sexual submission is pervasive in the sexual histories collected by this writer, and it is not a practice confined to working class blacks but equally represented among the bourgeoisie. While white men have always been able to use their superior economic resources to compel sexual submission from white women, there is increasing evidence that black men are not reluctant to use the prerequisites of high office or wealth to accomplish the same end.[20] Small wonder, then, that the black women in Johnson's college sample reported more negative feelings on the day following their first premarital sexual experience than their white counterparts.[21]

Although we recognize that much of the sexual behavior of black males is a function of forces beyond their control (i.e., white racism and internal colonialism) there must be some accountability for these individual actions. In every study comparing black and white sexuality, the great conflict between values and feelings exists among sex roles — not racial groups. Black and white men are much more united in the meaning of sex than are black men and black women. Men of both races are similar in the very selfish, peer-oriented nature of their sexual behavior.

THE USES OF SEX

A common tactic of men is to use sex as a control over women. A 31-year old female social worker spoke to this issue: "What bothers me is that the men I've met have not been satisfied with having sex but they want to control your mind as well. Some of them have believed that just because I went to bed with them, they have the right to dictate my life style. They want to control my movements, change my clothes and hair and alter my values. I find that many men become threatened when they see you living a liberated lifestyle; partly because they wonder what they can offer you."* It is not uncommon for men to withdraw sexual services as a way of denying affection to women. As long as the man gives and takes away sex when he wants, he is asserting a form of control over a woman who may otherwise be psychologically and economically independent.

Of course, it should be noted that sex occupies a unique place in black culture. Black males, for instance, have had a strong sexual orientation because the sexual conquest of women was considered a masculine trait. Since other symbols of masculinity have been denied them in the society, sexual prowess became a partial substitute for achievement in other areas. Thus, the black male who has a variety of premarital sexual experiences occupies a prestigious position in his peer group.

The misuse of sex is not confined to men. In this capitalistic society sex is frequently part of a profit and loss system rather than the genuine sharing of minds and bodies. There is no dearth of black women who have used sex as a punishment, a tease, or as currency. While much of male sexual jealousy is unwarranted and reflects their view of women as property, women aid in the development of this destructive emotion by the cunning ploy of keeping partners wondering whether they are faithful or not. The emerging and prevalent practice of women enjoying companionship with men who are labelled as "friends" has done nothing to arrest male tendencies toward sexual jealousy.

However, the lion's share of the burden for our sex role conflicts must be placed upon black males. While some black women give as much as they get, the system inherently favors men. With an effective sex ratio of three black women to every male, the females have little, if any bargaining power, where men have such a larger number of women from which to choose.[22] In a sense, black women often find themselves in the position of sexually auditioning for a meaningful relationship. After a number of tryouts, they may find a black male who is willing to make a commitment to them.

We should not be deluded, however, the sexual revolution and its rhetoric notwithstanding, into believing that black women have

---

* Quote comes from interview document in black singles study by the author.

been able to totally separate sex from love and commitment. The contemporary rhetoric of black female sexual liberation heard may be best explained by their need to avoid cognitive dissonance. When there is incompatability between act and belief, the individual must reduce the dissonance by altering her behavior or codes. Consequently, black women who are sexually active, of necessity, develop liberal views about their sexuality. But, this psychological compartmentalization has its limitations. In spite of their liberal sexual activity most black women are bargaining for a stable relationship. And, they are bargaining with men for whom commitment, as a priority is very low in their scheme of things. A perceptive analysis of this situation is given by a 39 year-old male writer:

> You can sleep with someone faster in the seventies than in the fifties and early 60's. I think the whole sexual culture is faster in that respect. But there's a curious contradiction because at the same time there is all this sexual hedonism most women seem to be looking for someone to settle down with, for a non-one-night stand, are looking, that is to say, for their man.*

The specific liberation of black female sexuality would have been a godsend had black men attempted to understand the nature of female sexuality in general. Once the gates to the female orifice were open, the male response was to take hold of the legacy of the past. Lovemaking was (and is) categorized as a physical act with male satisfaction as its ultimate end. Hence, we find black women decrying the fact that tenderness, communication and emotion are not present in the act of sexual intercourse. Too often the male does not reveal his deeper emotions to his partner because he views such revelation as a sign of weakness. When tenderness or affection is expressed, women complain, it is only as a prelude to sexual activity.

CASUALTIES OF THE SEXUAL REVOLUTION

Many black women have come to find that the sexual revolution was not their war. Obviously, the strict double standard no longer exists but it has been supplanted by more arbitrary male standards about how sexually liberated women can be. A woman who proclaims "extreme" sexual liberation still finds herself ranked as less than desirable for the position of wife or even of stable companion.

---

* Interview data collected from black singles study.

In a recent study of male sexuality, a team of researchers found that many young men still adhere to the old traditional values. A large number of them wanted their wives to be virgins.[23] While these were white men, Johnson found in her study of black males that they were more likely to have a double standard than the white males in the same sample.[24] This could, of course, mean that black men do not want a woman who is as sexually active as they are suggesting that sexually liberated black women may not be among the chosen.

Even black women who accept this situation often find less fulfillment in their sexual efforts. Lack of tender foreplay and other insensitivities are oft-expressed grievances. Failure to achieve orgasm is frequently attributed to the male's refusal to use any technique other than penile penetration and thrusts. Although oral stimulation or clitoral manipulation may be necessary to help a woman achieve orgasm, many black men have strong taboos against such practices. In one of the few studies on the subject, Hunt found only 35 percent of single black males versus 72 percent of white males had participated in cunnilingus in a given year. However, 48 percent of single black women had engaged in fellatio — indicating that many black men believe it is better to receive than to give.[25]

THE NEW SEXUAL REALITY

The aforementioned turn of events would have less import if not for the changing realities of the black community. As of 1980, a majority of black women between the ages of 20 − 45 are not married or living with a spouse.[26] Reasons for this unprecedented situation range from the serious shortage of black males to increasing disenchantment with marriage as an institution. Whatever the reason, it is clear that this situation requires some rethinking of old values and practices. Many black women acquire extensive sexual experience because they realize it is impractical to wait for the elusive goal of marriage. The changing definitions of sex roles will also affect the sexual assertiveness of women and the expectations of male sexual performance. Blacks will have to be open to the variety of sexual expressions if their needs are to be filled in the context of the new black reality.

Whereas moral boundaries will have to be expanded to accommodate the new reality, some parameters must be maintained in order to preserve the black family. One of them may be an off-limits rule on those blacks who are currently married, since it has become fashionable for sexually liberated black women to include married men as sexual partners. Such extra-marital relationships might be acceptable if they remained merely physical relationships but they run the constant danger of becoming emotional ones which could disrupt existing marriages. In 1980, 26.6 percent of the black population between the ages of 25 and 54 were divorced compared to only 8.4 percent among whites.[27] Some of this statistical and racial disparity may be attributed to the pressure exerted by single black women entangled with married men. The same parameters should be applied to married women, though they are generally less accessible, and for different reasons, than male spouses.

The continuing shortage of black men will pose a dilemma for many black women. A common suggestion made, mostly by men, is that women should be willing to share their men (i.e., polygamy).[28] Such multiple relationships could be viable if men were also willing to share and if women who had internalized values of monogamy could accept such an arrangement. In most cases they can not, especially when the sharing must be acknowledged and agreed upon. The defacto sharing that now exists has been responsible for its share of heartbreak, jealousy, violence and mental anguish.

Concomitant with the sexual revolution and the new reality, blacks must be accepting of the right of women to choose whether they wish to bear children or not. That means making available safe contraceptives and access to abortions on demand. Because of the unsafe nature of many female contraceptives, males must take greater responsibility for birth control. The male virility cult must be abandoned and be replaced by sensitive males, who are willing to use condoms or undergo vasectomies after siring a reasonable number of children. Since some black women may remain single all their lives they may choose to adopt a child or to have one out-of-wedlock. Such alternatives should be permissible within the expanded moral boundaries necessary to cope with our new reality.

This critical analysis of black sexuality should not be allowed to overshadow the positive aspects of the sexual lives of blacks. In the main, blacks continue to engage in and enjoy their sexual encounters. Part of the problem arises from the conflict of traditional values with new realities. And, for the bourgeoisie, these values were not black values. This does not mean that the black sexual experience has been a bleak or negative one. For the most part, sex has been the one haven black people have had from the daily oppression of white racism.

SUMMARY

The psychological burden has fallen heavily on black men. Denied equal access to the prosaic symbols of mahood, they manifest their masculinity in the most extreme form of sexual domination. When they have been unable to achieve status in the workplace, they have exercised the privilege of their manliness and attempted to achieve it in the bedroom. Feeling a constant need to affirm their masculinity, tenderness and compassion are eschewed as signs of weakness. which leave them vulnerable to the ever-feared possibility of female domination. These feelings arise out of the differential socialization of men and women into sexual behavior. Until recently, these differences were consensually ratified by the black community. But, the sexual revolution and subsequent new black reality has created additional problems of ambiguity for them. The absence of clear definitions as to what is expected of the sexes in intimate relationships has made interpersonal conflict the dominant motif of male-female interaction.

For some black men, the internalization of racist sexual beliefs has led to a different response, one of preoccupation with their sexual prowess and the neglect of their many other talents. The mass media has collaborated in this process by its own emphasis on the superstud qua pimp in movies, on television, and in popular literature. Such a situation has predictable consequences when the sexually reluctant black female encounters the hypersexualized black male. Conflict ensues as an accommodation between their antagonistic sexual orientations becomes difficult to attain. The fragility of many black male-female relationships is partially a reflection of this unresolved subterranean war between black

women who are sexually unresponsive and black men who are sexually exploitative. A black sexuality which could exist without the
constraints of white-inspired stereotypes would be a healthier form
of behavior.

I am neither advocating nor endorsing non-traditional sexual
practices. Those people who engage in them will do so on the basis
of their own compelling circumstances and needs. Choosing to do
so should not make them pariahs in the black community. Freedom of choice is an inviolate right which should not be abrogated
by the irrational prejudices of others. Alternative sexual lifestyles
should not be allowed to become a divisive issue while the struggle
for freedom is still at hand. But a cessation of the sexual conflict
which threatens to tear the black community asunder is needed,
nonetheless.

It is not the sexual revolution but the new black reality that com-
mands our attention. For the first time in our history the majority
of black women, and large numbers of men, are and will remain
unmarried. Perforce, their sexuality must be harnessed in such a
way as to promote the gratification of this universal human need.
Sex should be used as a means of communication, not as an instrument of domination and control. The time for game playing is
over. Both men and women must cultivate modalities of healthy
sexual expression which will preserve their basic integrity and
humanity. As for the question of black "sexual superiority," we do
not need this label any more than we have heretofore needed the
appellation of "mental inferiority." Above all, a sexual ethos is
needed that will contribute racial unity, and that value system
must serve all the people of the black community.

CHAPTER SIX:

Homosexuality and the Black Male

Male friendships were regarded once by Aristotle as the most perfect of friendships. Indeed, masculine friendships were the only ones that he considered, with the exception of a brief allusion to the possibility of friendship between husband and wife. The average woman, in ancient Greece, was regarded as too ignorant, intellectually, to be capable of deep friendship with anyone.[1] The present state of male friendships is far from what Aristotle celebrated. According to other research studies and my own, single males have fewer meaningful friendships than most women, with either sex. A couple of reasons for the differences are clear. Women are more likely to be socialized into a nurturant role that complements the friendship role than are men who maintain a certain emotional distance from other men due to the fear of being labeled homosexual or weak.[2]

Homosexuality is the most difficult behavior of blacks to trace historically. Wherever social contact between persons of the same sex has existed, there has probably been some homosexual behavior. In pre-colonial Africa there was traditionally a division of labor, separate initiation training for males and females, in addition to economic and socio-political associations organized along gender lines. The practice, for instance, of some African tribes of sending young male children off to separate compounds may have produced some homosexual behavior. Such practices are rarely noted in the literature on African society. Instead, a noted Africanist asserts: "Although no proper studies of the problem have been made in traditional African societies, homosexual practices

87

seem to be rare, or only confined to boys and girls before marriage. Part of the reason for this is that the psychological atmosphere from childhood to adolescence prepares one towards the goal of marriage, and a person, therefore directs his sexual development towards relationship with the opposite sex."[3]

One of the effects of the sexual revolution is the increase in "visible" homosexuality. It is one area in the changing of sexual values that has significant black participation. However, the increase in people assuming overtly gay lifestyles is largely confined to black males. It is not known how many people in the United States are exclusively homosexual, but estimates range from 5 to 20 percent of the total population. The nation's prisons are the main places where homosexual preferences are evident. Some black men who acquired their homosexual behavior as prison inmates because of the unavailability of women continue it after their release. Their reasons for turning to homosexual lifestyles vary, ranging from a desire to escape family responsibilities to acquiring money through prostitution. An interesting side aspect of the sexual revolution is the development in San Francisco of "gay liberation" groups that are so politically powerful that few politicians dare run for office without seeking their support.

Despite a shortage of black males, relatively few black women have joined the community as overt lesbians. But since female homosexuals are not as visible as male homosexuals, the number of black lesbians is difficult to determine. As with the black male homosexual, many black lesbians are deeply involved in the white homosexual community.

It is not known whether homosexuality is more or less prevalent in the black population than in the white because there is little data available on the subject for blacks. Some writers have claimed that blacks have a greater incidence of male homosexuality than whites. The reason for their belief is that female-headed households in the black community have resulted in a lack of male role models for male black children.[4] However there is no evidence to support this supposition.

After placing obstacles to self realization in the way of the black male, America then has its bearers of ideology, the social scientists, falsely indict him for his lack of manhood. There are various sociological and psychological studies which purport to show how black males are de-masculinized, and suggest in fact, that they may be latent homosexuals. The reason cited is that black males reared in female-centered households are more likely to acquire feminine characteristics because there is no consistent adult male model or image to shape their personalities.[5] One sociologist stated that since black males are unable to enact the masculine role, they tend to cultivate their personalities. In this respect they resemble women who use their personalities to compensate for their inferior status in relation to men.[6]

If the above reasoning seems weak and unsubstantiated, the other studies of black emasculation are equally feeble. Many of the hypotheses about the effeminate character of black men are based on their scores on the Minnesota Multiphasic Inventory Test (MMPI), a psychological instrument that asks the subject to determine how over five hundred simple statements apply to him. Black males score higher than white males on the section which measures femininity. As an indicator of their femininity, the researchers cite the fact that black men more often agreed with such feminine choices as "I would like to be a singer" and "I think I feel more intensely than most people do."[7]

This is the kind of evidence that the dominant society has marshalled to prove the feminization of the black male. The only thing this demonstrates is that white standards cannot always be used in evaluating black behavior. Black people live in another environment, with different ways of thinking, acting and believing from the white, middle class world. Singers such as James Brown and others represent successful role models in the black community. Black male youths aspire to be singers because this appears to be an observable means for obtaining success in this country — not because they are more feminine than white males. In addition, music is an integral part of black culture.

As part of their studies of sexual deviants, the Kinsey group investigated black homosexuality. They found that black men were more comfortable around homosexuals and did not perceive them as any kind of threat to their manhood. Consequently, black homosexuals (male and female) were not as isolated from the black heterosexual population. They were not relegated to their own bars or social cliques. Also, blacks were more likely to be bi-sexual than exclusively homosexual.[8]

THE SEXUAL SOLUTION

Finding a sexual partner is not a crucial or pervasive problem for many black singles, especially women. Achieving regular sexual gratification within the context of an emotionally satisfying relationship is. One alternative lifestyle that purports to resolve this problem is that of homosexuality. I realize the difficulty of positing this behavioral modality as an alternative to conventional marriage, still it is an option that is being discussed and, in some cases, adopted. Whether the increased visibility of homosexuality is due to the shortage of black men or to the conflict in male/female relationships, we do not know; however about 20 of the men we interviewed are homosexual or bisexual. These findings are part of a larger study of 500 black, college educated singles, of whom approximately 110 are males. These findings also could be due to the fact that all our interviews, and a large proportion of the questionnaires, come from the San Francisco Bay Area. In San Francisco itself gays constitute an estimated 25 percent of the adult population. We interviewed no known lesbians and our attempts to include them in the study were unsuccessful. Each quote, unless identified or footnoted comes from my black singles data.

Homosexuality is difficult to discuss as an option for black singles because it remains a subject fraught with controversy. Even understanding the nature of homosexuality is problematic because the research is permeated by bias. On the one hand, there are those who consider homosexuality to be a genetic disorder and everyone affected by it to be a pervert. More recently, there are those who declare homosexuals to be similar to heterosexuals in order to enhance the civil rights of gays. Some would claim that homosexuality cannot be a viable alternative for black singles because that tendency is formed in early childhood. However, we are in agreement with psychiatrist Richard Green who suggests that "at the present time the most one can say about the genesis of homosexuality is that it remains unknown."[9] In interpreting the importance of sexual orientation we might keep in mind the words of Erich Fromm: "the very first thing we notice about anybody is whether that person is male or female. And its the one thing we never forget. Name, telephone number, profession, politics, all of these details may slip from our memory, but never the individual's sex."[10] Therefore our sexual preference, linked together, is an important source of a person's identity.

Not only have we failed to understand the causes of homosexuality, but we still know little about its nature. It is estimated that 10 percent of the male population is homosexual. Although no reliable figures are available, blacks are assumed to be proportionally representative in that gay population. The majority of gays are assumed to be male, but lesbians maintain a low profile and are less likely to reveal themselves. It appears that the majority of black homosexuals, both men and women, have less than a college education, although they are well represented, or perhaps more visible, in certain middle class occupations. Many live in urban locales where the possibility of discovery is less likely, although they can be found in all environments. Certainly those involved in an openly gay lifestyle live in large cities with sizeable gay populations. Today the most hospitable cities for them in the United States are New York, Los Angeles and San Francisco.

BLACK MALE HOMOSEXUALS

A recent study entitled *Homosexualities* by Bell and Weinberg has attempted to refute some of the stereotypes about gays. Their book provides the source for most of our information about black homosexuals. In general they found that black male homosexuals tend to be younger than their white counterparts, with an average age of 27 in contrast to 37 for white males. They had less education and were employed at a lower occupational level than white gays. Members of the black group more often expressed the belief that their homosexuality and homosexual contacts had helped more than hurt their careers. Over two-thirds of black male gays reported they spent less than half of their leisure time by themselves in comparison to half of their white brethren. Both the black and white homosexual men claimed to have more good, close friends than the heterosexual men did. A similar difference existed in attitudes about job satisfaction. Black and white homosexuals expressed greater satisfaction with their jobs than did heterosexual men. About half of the black and white male homosexuals stated they had no regret whatsoever about being homosexual.[11]

It is worth noting that only one fourth of the black gay males said that all their friends were men.[12] The other gays probably constitute a large proportion of the platonic male friends many single women have. They make very good friends for many of these women because they share some of the same interests and they do not view women as sexual objects. A 26 year old gay male artist said:

> I enjoy women a lot. I enjoy their companionship without emotional entanglements. I prefer having a platonic relationship with a woman rather than a man. Most of my male friends are gay and our interests overlap too much and we become competitive. I go out to dinners, movies, museums, plays and talk on the telephone with my female friends. They help me keep things in perspective and provide me with a balance to my life. However, they tend to lament the fact that I'm a man lost to them.

Another interesting characteristic of the black gay lifestyle is the extent of their involvement with whites. Over two thirds of the black male homosexuals said that half of their sexual partners had been white.[13] One of our respondents believed race was less important in the gay community. However, he acknowledged that whatever their sexual orientation, whites still have a certain insensitivity to blacks and cultural differences present problems. One black male gay declared that the majority of whites who are homosexually interested in blacks are misfits, that they desire a black mate only because they sense an identity between their own feelings of inferiority and the myth of black inferiority.[14] Whatever the reason, there is certainly some element of racism among white homosexuals. As a black male homosexual reported:

> I've learned that in San Francisco's gay bars there's real racism — even overt racism — in terms of just being able to get in gay bars. They ask black gays for three pieces of I.D. with their pictures on them, but they don't ask whites for that. Or, they have a certain quota and after they've filled it, they won't let any Third World people in. And there are still the sexual myths about black people. The myth of the black man as a stud, for example.

Some non-white homosexuals began to confront the racism in gay bars in San Francisco. Since bars are the center of social life for gays, the exclusion of non-whites was of more than passing significance. In November, 1980, more than 20 non-white gays demonstrated in front of a San Francisco gay bar, charging racial discrimination against minority gays. According to a spokesman for the Gay Democratic Club, "Gay bar owners think its bad for business to encourage minority gay patrons."[15] In the same city a rift is growing between the straight black community and white gays over the increasing displacement of black tenants by gays who are purchasing and renovating homes in the black ghettos. While the practice, known as "gentrification," is a commonplace practice in other cities, the large number of gays buying up homes in black neighborhoods has intensified black hostility to them and created speculation that most low-income blacks will be moved out of the city in a few years.

If black homosexuals stay in the black community they do not necessarily find a high degree of acceptance. Blacks may tolerate but will not openly approve of homosexual behavior. Ministers in the black church have preached that it is unnatural for men to burn for men, and women to burn for women. The A.M.E. church is on record as being strongly opposed to homosexuality.[16] Black physicians have tried to "cure" homosexuality in black patients. A Howard University newspaper called gays "freaks" and condemned the practice as capitalist depravity.[17] However, black male homosexuals were less likely to hide the fact of their homosexuality from their family and friends than their white counterparts.[18] As one black gay reported, "In a lot of ways the black community won't accept homosexuals, but, in a lot of ways I feel blacks will accept gays before the white community does — on a gut level — simply because blacks know what it's like to be oppressed."

Lack of approval by the black community, moreover, is not the only problem faced by male homosexuals. Sexual contacts are often fleeting ones, with one third of the men reported having had at least 500 different sexual partners during the course of their homosexual careers.[19] Despite those large numbers, two thirds of them complained of having trouble finding a suitable sexual partner.[20] Just as in the heterosexual world, youth and attractiveness are highly valued. Most younger gay men tended to rate their sex appeal higher than the older men did.[21] As one young gay male commented, "I hope I don't live much past 50. After that, nobody wants to look at you, and you always have to pay for sex." There was an interesting racial difference between the psychological adjustment of black and white male homosexuals, with the black males more likely to feel less happy at the present time than they did five years ago, to feel more tension and to feel lonely more frequently.[22]

With all these problems, homosexuality seems to be no trouble-free alternative, at least not for black males. Coupled with the stigma is the fact that many problems heterosexuals face are present in the homosexual world. Among them are the problems of finding a compatible partner. A number of gay males complained they were unable to find a compatible male with whom to establish a meaningful relationship. One male, a 35 year-old social worker told us:

> Yes, I've lived with a lover in a homosexual relationship. The first four years were wonderful but the last six months were hell. I'm basically a relationship person. But the society reinforces butterfly relationships, where you light one second for sex. He wanted to continue living together but I wasn't willing. He was conventionally middle class while I'm more bohemian. He cares what people think and I don't.

BLACK LESBIANS

Lesbians share the social stigma of their gay male counterparts but there are significant differences between the two groups. One of the reasons that lesbians are less visible could be attributed to the possibility that they are less socially acceptable in the black community. So thinks Audre Lorde, who declares: "If the recent hysterical rejection of lesbians in the black community is based solely upon an aversion to the idea of sexual contact between members of the same sex — why then is the idea of sexual contact between black men so much more easily accepted, or unremarked."[23] Another black lesbian speaks thus about her oppression:

> As a black lesbian I am in a weird situation. I am oppressed not only by society as a whole, but the black community too. The black community looks upon the lesbian as blacks do upon whites. This is particularly true of black males who consider lesbians a threat. Black males think that a lesbian is fair game sexually for anybody, because she can't get a man or is turned off by men.[24]

Those black women who chose lesbianism fared better than

their male counterparts. They had fewer transient sexual contacts, for example, most of them had fewer than ten female sexual partners during the course of their homosexual careers and two-thirds of them reported that the majority of their sexual partners had been persons whom they cared about and for whom they had some affection.[25] In the lesbian culture, youthfulness did not carry the importance it had among male homosexuals or heterosexuals. Because members of the same sex are more sensitive to each other's sexual needs, many lesbians reported satisfactory sexual experiences. This was most evident in the fact that lesbians displayed greater skill in performing oral sex than did men engaged in performing oral sex with women.[26] Fewer than two-thirds of the black lesbians reported that they spent less than half of their leisure time alone.[27] Few of the lesbians encountered sexual problems or contracted a veneral disease.[28] However, black lesbians were more likely to report poorer health and more psychosomatic symptoms, to feel lonely more often, and to display more tension and paranoia.[29]

We know no more about the causes of lesbianism than we do about male homosexuality. A theory that covers both groups is that their homosexual orientation emerges in response to past difficulties in heterosexual relationships. It is true that a half of the black lesbians had been married at least once (compared to fewer than 20 percent of black male homosexuals.)[30] And some black female singles in our study reported that they had considered a lesbian relationship if their relationship with men did not improve.

According to a 37 year-old teacher: "I'm not ready for homosexuality yet. If men keep playing games with me, I might consider switching in later life. Right now, I still know a few cool dudes." Probably a more typical response to lesbianism is that of a 39 year-old college administrator:

> Don't worry about me and the Daughters of Bilitis. Somehow I don't think deliberately complicating my life like that would net me anything I'm particularly in need of. For that kind of risk I'd have to be *assured* of something really great. Knowing what I know about human beings of both sexes and many races I have little hope that anybody can assure me of anything. So, I'll take my chances with my present lifestyle.

Indications are that most black women live primarily heterosexual lives. Some have recently turned to occasional bisexual experiences. Most of them do this in a clandestine manner, frequently between their serious relationships with men. Some have claimed that there is no such thing as bisexuality, only people who are basically homosexual with the ability to perform heterosexually. But our interviews with psychologists, leaders of women's groups and gay black males confirm a great deal of alternation between partners of different sexual orientations. A number of women reported having sexual experiences with men who were regarded as exclusively homosexual. Some of the women in our sample were formerly married to men who eventually came out of the closet. During the marriage they claimed to have experienced a normal frequency of sex relations. One of our male subjects, a 37 year-old professor said:

> I have considered an alternative lifestyle involving a male partner as well as legal marriage to a woman. I feel that I could do either and be happy. I prefer to do it with a woman for awhile because I would like children — perhaps later with a man. I'm too conservative to do the both together.

Such an attitude has led some observers of the homosexual scene to speculate that homosexuality is nothing more than a trendy fad. They believe that some black males become homosexuals in order to take advantage of the gay network to gain access to better jobs and other perquisites of homosexuality. Considering the continued liabilities of being gay, such an explanation lacks much credibility. Another reason is given by feminist Michelle Wallace, who observes that, "I don't think that all of these people that are homosexual out here were born that way. I think that men and women are having a lot of problems now with each other and sometimes they think the easiest way to get around that is to go with the same sex: but of course, the same problems appear, because they're having problems with themselves and with people in general."[31]

SUMMARY

Whenever men come into contact, homosexual behavior is a possible outcome. Sometimes it may be temporary activity, such as during the gender exclusive adolescence years, in prisons and among military men. In such cases, homosexual activity is time-contained, a function of the absence of women. American society inadvertently encourages homosexuality by the organization of gender-linked associations. Sports activity, for example, may lead to homosexuality because it brings men together in a common event from which women are largely excluded. According to one anthropologist, the aspects of male bonding in the game makes "football a form of ritualized homosexuality. All the physical expression taboos in American society are converted in football into acceptable behavior — fanny patting — and symbolically the very structure of the game."[32]

As for the morality of homosexual behavior, that is not a judgment for this writer or the society to make. There is no reason to judge more harshly the behavior of men in private places than to judge any other deviation from the norm. Certainly it is behavior that has survived the years and constraints on its expression. And, many of our most admired and creative leaders have engaged in it. Recognizing the rights of homosexuals to lead their lives in peace, however, does not preclude the speculation that men indulge in it for a variety of motives, not all of them positive, and that problems exist in the internal structure of the homosexual community.

Part IV:
Male/Female Relationships

CHAPTER SEVEN

Black Men/Black Women: Changing Roles and Relationships

The decade of the seventies was witness to a number of changes in marriage and the family. Considering the sanctity of the nuclear family as an American institution, the changes that transpired were only short of revolutionary. In 1979 almost half of the women in the 20 to 24 year-old age bracket were still single, compared with only 28 percent in 1960. Even in the later years, 25 to 29, 20 percent of them remained unmarried in 1979. During the period 1970 to 1979, the ratio of divorced persons per 1,000 husbands and wives in intact marriages increased by 96 percent from 47 per 1,000 to 92 per 1,000.[1] As startling as these figures may be, they do not begin to mirror the changes in single and marital status and fertility behavior among the Afro-American population. The majority of Afro-Americans, over the age of 18, are no longer in intact marriages. About 47 percent of black men and 56 percent of black women are not married and living with a spouse. Almost half (48.7 percent) of all black families are headed by a single parent. The majority of black children are born out-of-wedlock and only a minority of black children live in a two-parent household.[2] Thus, at the end of the seventies, the black family had undergone a radical transformation. The nuclear family is no longer the assumed structure. This fact raises the question of why and how the transformation occurred.

It is clear that the white American family is changing in the same direction but the magnitude of these changes have been much greater for black Americans. Seemingly, blacks have come almost full circle to the period of slavery when marriage was denied them.

However, after the demise of "the peculiar institution," they married in record numbers. By the beginning of the twentieth century three out of four adult blacks were members of a nuclear family. About 90 percent of all black children were born in wedlock during that same period.[3] Even in the more recent era, black women over 65 years of age had a higher rate of marriage (96.5) than comparable white women (93.1).[4] Historically, a legal marriage was employed as a device by which status was determined. Blacks were considered respectable or non-respectable based on whether they were legally married or cohabitating. My guess is that the black American's desire to be in a nuclear family has not changed but the conditions which permit fulfillment of that desire have been altered significantly.

BLACK SINGLES

The increase in black singles is consistent with the constraints on the supply of eligible mates available for and interested in a monogamous marriage. Not only is there an excess of one million adult black women (over age 18) in the black population but the institutional decimation of black men leaves working class black women with an extremely low supply of desirable men (i.e. employed and mentally stable) from which to choose. This is particularly true of men who reach the age of thirty and are single or divorced. Paradoxically, there is a larger number of never-married black men at lower class levels than there are similar black women.[5] In the lower classes, these men are without skills, education and a steady income. Thus, it makes sense in terms of daily economic security for black women to avoid a legal marriage with such men. They may live with these men and have children by them; but, as one black women asserted: "Without marriage I know I've got security. My welfare check keeps coming as long as I am not married. Otherwise I don't know if he's going to keep his job or if he's going to start "acting up" and staying out drinking and fooling around with other women. This way I might not have the respectability of marriage, but at least I know how much I got."

Many of the stable black marriages are among couples in the black working class. These are the blacks who finished high school but have less than four years of college. The men in this group tend to be dependent on the wife's income to maintain a decent standard of living. Because they avoid the harsh economic repression of black males in the underclass, it seems easier for them to maintain a stable marriage and average standard of living. Often, they are the "silent majority," the men who are unrepresented in the literature and general stereotypes about black males.

When we ascend the socio-economic scale, the men between the ages 35 to 54 years[6] in the middle class are more likely to remain single than their female counterparts, at least those with five years of college or more. Many of those men are exclusive homosexuals, for whom a legal marriage is not possible.

Among the black middle class, (i.e. 4 years of college or more) the shortage of black males is complicated by a number of factors. Assuming a woman wants to marry a male of comparable education, there were only 339,000 black male college graduates for 417,000 black female college graduates in 1977. Moreover, the eligible pool of college educated black men is further reduced by homosexuality, interracial marriages and the fact that many of them marry women with less than a college education. As a result, among blacks (ages 35–54) with 5 years or more of college, there are 52,000 eligible women for only 15,000 men. To illustrate the seriousness of the problem, the census bureau lists 15,000 divorced black women in that same category and *no* black males (actually less than 500).[7] Small wonder, then, that competition among black women is keen for that low supply of college educated black males. And, it is the competition for those men that largely explains their high divorce rate. The marriages of these black males often are disrupted by "the other woman." We see it in the statistics which show that black women are more likely than white women to marry men who are four and more years their senior and who have been married before.[8]

THE COST OF BEING MALE AND SINGLE

It is commonplace to hear of families cutting back on expenses to cope with the increasing cost of goods and services. Reducing their expenditures is easily accomplished among married couples since they perceive themselves as an inseparable unit with the same goals. But, there is another group whose expenses continue to rise.

This group consists of individuals whom we typically refer to as the swinging single men. Among blacks, they are more than a crowd — they are almost the majority of adult black men. As of 1979, almost half of the black men, ages 18 and above, had never been married, or are separated, divorced or widowed. Approximately 47 percent of adult black men and 56 percent of comparable black women are eligible for the "take-out, make-out" game known as dating.[9] Yet due to age, poverty, children, or lack of opportunity, the majority of black singles do not go out on dates — at least not very often.

Dating, in fact, is a relatively new concept to most blacks. Prior to the desegregation of public facilities, there were few places to go. Most blacks met in the church, school or neighborhood, and spent leisurely evenings sitting on their front porchs. Marriage followed soon afterwards. Presently, blacks are more likely to remain unmarried for a longer period of time, especially those who are considered middle class. Almost a third of the black women who go to college remain unmarried past the age of thirty. Men with the same educational background tend to marry at an earlier age but a high divorce rate throws many of them back into the singles world.[10] And, the purpose of dating has changed. No longer is it solely a form of courtship, especially for men, where each person's intent is to explore the potential for marriage or a stable relationship. Some still use it to serve that function. However, a large number of men and women view it as recreation, a free night's entertainment, a time for sexual seduction and status enhancement.

While the purpose of dating has changed considerably the roles have not altered that much. Men are still expected to bear the costs of dating. Why this tradition continues to exist is somewhat of a mystery. Few college educated black women live at home with their parents, bereft of any visible means of support and in fact, college educated black women earn 90 percent of the income of their male peers. One answer is that it is a self-serving interpretation of a custom designed for an earlier era and it is one that has been largely unaffected by the women's liberation movement. It is a sacrosanct tradition with a great deal of force behind it. Men who violate that tradition are labelled as cheap. The ability to escort a woman in style is often the measure of the man, especially in this inflationary period. Dr. Joyce Brothers once commented that when economic times are hard, women look for signs of a man's socioeconomic status. When we were in a period of economic prosperity, women were attracted to men with sex appeal as exhibited in snappy apparel such as tight-fitting pants and open chested shirts. Now, it is the three piece suit, signaling arrival, which turns women on.

For middle class black men, appealing to women can be an expensive proposition. The higher status clothes and car can be very expensive outlays. Most good quality suits cost at least $500. The "right" kind of car (e.g. Porsche, BMW, Mercedes) sells for twenty thousand dollars and above. Since the initial attraction of the sexes to each other is based on external, visible factors, those accoutrements are necessary. A man's possession of money is important but not as important as his willingness to spend it. One black woman, a 33 year old college professor, once called a man she dated "cheap." When asked why, she cited the case of their initial meeting at a bar where she sat with three female companions. After ordering a drink and talking to them for a period of time, the bill for $34 arrived. To their surprise, he insisted on paying only for his own drink and not picking up the entire tab.

The more formal dating situations can be quite expensive. An investment counselor, Ray Devoe has constructed a "cost of loving index." Using 1954 as his base year, he calculated that the cost of dating has increased twice as much as the advance in the consumer price index — 340 percent vs. 172 percent. And, the cost of an average date is now about $43.[11] Of course, it can be higher or lower, depending on the choice of activity and location. Since women may judge men on their willingness to spend, a "cheap date" may be costly. There is a cadre of women who do not know any cheap forms of entertainment and an equal number who do not appreciate them. As one woman, a 34 year old nurse, told me: "the one time you don't worry about being on a diet is when a man is picking up the tab." And, how many men look first at the prices on a restaurant menu and multiply by two before they consider a choice of food? Going out to eat is often necessary since many younger black women (southern women being an exception) do not know how to cook. A man living in the expensive urban centers such as New York, Boston, Washington, and San Francisco, and planning on going to the theatre, having dinner and drinks, must also figure on paying $100 for the night. As the investment counselor has noted, "the dating game doesn't come cheap. And, carried to an excess, it can quickly bankrupt you."[12]

There are several anticipated consequences of the cost of dating. As many women reported to me, they do not get many invitations for dates. Some men go out with other men and split expenses down the middle. It is not uncommon to go to concerts, plays, restaurants and see men grouped with men, women with women and some men alone. Another common complaint of the women was that men simply dropped by their homes and wanted to watch television, get high or otherwise hang out. As one woman reported to me, "the only place men ever took me was from the living room into the bedroom."* And that is yet another consequence of the rising cost of dating. Men become sexually aggressive faster because they cannot afford to prolong dating for an extended period of time. One man, a 37 year old lawyer, told me: "I can't see taking a woman out and spending $50 for the night's entertainment. There was this one woman whose taste ran to French restaurants. Not only did she order the most expensive dish on the menu and a bottle of expensive wine but I even had to pay for the Perrier she ordered. After getting the bill for $89, I was determined to get some reward for my money." Such an attitude led one woman, a 32 year old social worker to ask the question: "Are women expected to screw for their supper? All a man gets for taking me out is the 'pleasure of my company.'"

Considering the cost of dating, only a certain category of men can and will engage in it for long periods of time. A noticeable trend is toward women in their twenties and thirties dating men in their late forties and early fifties. When I asked one woman, a 32 year old specialist in multi-cultural education, why she dated so many men in their forties, she replied: "because you don't have to pick up the tab for your own dinner. They come from the old

---

* Unless otherwise identified or footnoted, quotes are taken from the black singles data. See chapter six for a description of the study.

school and know how to treat a woman. Besides, they know if they want to date a woman 15 years their junior, they have to spend money on her." These older men, of course, are often at the peak of their earning power, some are recently divorced and new to the dating game. Also, some men are in positions where they can write off the costs of dating on expense accounts or as tax deductions.

Women, however, are not spared the expense of dating or finding a man. Since a man's willingness to spend money on her is often based on how attractive she is, she must lay out fairly large sums of money for cosmetics, hairstyling and fashionable clothes. Since fashions in clothes and hairstyles fluctuate almost yearly, they are a considerable expense for her.[13] Moreover, many women incur the costs of going to places in order to meet men. Even if a woman goes with a girlfriend to a bar or club, she generally pays her own way. Then, there is the conference circuit. Some women save their pennies all year in order to attend the annual meetings of the National Medical or Bar Association, and as a result, many predominantly black conferences have a disproportionate number of women in attendance, in relationship to their numbers in the profession. Most of the men, however, are married and, therefore, "single for the conference only."

Hence, dating is not just a case of men paying and women receiving. Furthermore, as men and women enter into stable relationships, they often stay home together or she invites him over to dinner. And, there are increasing instances of women sharing the cost of the evenings entertainment. Ann Arbor, Michigan, a college town, was the only city where this seemed to be the norm. After having coffee with a young woman there, I picked up the bill for $1.10 and she asked if I wanted her to pay for her cup of coffee. When I said no, she replied that you had to do that in Ann Arbor since the men were quick to pick out the cost of their meal and pay only that amount. Possibly Ann Arbor's practice may be the harbinger of the future. If not, the cost of dating in the future will have outpriced most black men. Based on my own calculations, a man who remains single and "dates" steadily for twenty years can expect to spend almost $75,000 for dating alone.

There are a few other costs that blacks must pay for all the singles in their midst. In the past, many black families maintained a decent or middle class standard of living through the double wages of both husband and wife. Since there are no longer as many black husband/wife couples, the standard of living has decreased for blacks. According to the Bureau of the Census report, between 1976 and 1978, the proportion of black families with two or more earners declined from 48 to 46 percent. The proportion of white families with two or more earners remained at 55 percent. While that may be attributed to a decline in the employment status of black women, only 48 percent of the adult black women were reported as married and living with a spouse in 1976. That was a considerable decline from the 66 percent who were married, with spouse present, in 1950. The difference that marriage makes is illustrated in the figures that show black husband/wife families (husband under 35 years old), in the North and West, in which both spouses were earners and achieved incomes equal to those of their white peers in 1976. On the other hand, the median income of the black family (which includes single parent households) declined from 60 percent of white family income in 1974 to 57 percent in 1977.[14]

Unmarried blacks who share the American dream of owning their own home may have to forget it. Presently, the average home seems to be available only to two wage families. According to recent surveys, over 54 percent of home buyers relied on two incomes to buy a house in 1979. And, among first time buyers, those families in which the wife was employed accounted for 64 percent of the total.[15] Few single blacks have the income required to meet the monthly mortgage payments for most new homes. Ironically, it is, in part, the dramatic increase in the number of singles that accounts for the rapid rise in housing prices.[16] In the last decade the number of households increased more than twice as fast as the number of people in them. In 1978, more than half of all households consisted on only one or two individuals. In other words, the housing that used to accommodate a husband/wife couple must now be doubled to house the unmarried individual.

Interestingly enough, it may also be economic factors that will stem the tide of increasing singleness. More and more blacks seem to be gravitating toward marriage this year. Certainly inflationary trends combined with a economic recession have forced many of them to seek the security of a stable relationship as opposed to a casual dating lifestyle. Women used to seek security in marriages, then began to seek it in jobs. As the job picture, especially for blacks, became more bleak and uncertain, they are again looking to marriage for security. Another factor is that the high cost of dating insures only the most attractive women (and sometimes not them) a steady pool of men willing to bear those expenses. Perforce, many black women are remaining at home alone or going out primarily with other women. Dating may be an idea whose time has come and gone.

Many blacks will continue to remain unmarried due to demographic factors. There remains in the black community an imbalance in the sex ratio, resulting from the institutional decimation of black men, who cannot get jobs and who wind up on drugs, in the military or prison or dead at a young age. The black singles world is characterized by a large proportion of men who are uneducated, with low incomes, and an equally disproportionate number of women with college degrees and high incomes. Until some of our values change, it is evident that few of the former will be dating the latter. As has often been the case, economics is a strong determinant of one's marital status.

UNFAITHFUL WOMEN AND JEALOUS MEN

After hunger and sex, sexual jealousy is one of the strongest passions experienced by homo sapiens. Jealousy does not exist in every culture and emerged in Western culture as a result of the development of private property.[17] Certainly it is a common emotion among Americans. Jealousy of one's mate is a major cause of marital disruption and interpersonal violence. It is such a destructive emotion that therapists generally attempt to label it as a pathological state of mind. Various theories attribute jealousy to low self-esteem, misanthropy, personal unhappiness, etc. While it seems obvious that much jealousy is irrational, we rarely hear about rational jealousy and the social forces that promote jealousy. If absolute fidelity is required from a mate, what are the chances that it will be given? In today's society, the chances are fairly low. This fact will give rise to jealous suspicions that are unfounded in particular but true in general. Hence, it is incumbent upon us to examine infidelity as well as sexual jealousy in order to understand their relationship to one another.

Although little has been written about it, sexual jealousy is not unknown in the black community. Indeed, one study found that 40 percent of blacks, whose marriages had terminated, gave as at least one of the reasons, often as the only reason, jealousy and infidelity.[18] One pronounced difference in black jealousy is that these suspicious attitudes are not that uncommon to men. In the same study previously cited, black men felt that a wife would search for sexual gratification elsewhere if relations did not go well.[19] And, that belief is confirmed in the findings of Bell that almost half of his black female subjects believed that a married woman would be justified in running around.[20] The Rainwater study found that 31 percent of the divorced women in the survey admitted to at least one extramarital affair.[21] In another study of college-educated black divorcees, 54 percent believed that their ex-husbands had engaged in extramarital sexual activity.[22]

It must be emphasized that infidelity per se is seldom the cause of divorce, especially when women terminate the marriage. Lower income women may divorce a man who is unfaithful *and* also fails to support his family. Both violations of societal norms may be too much for her to bear. Among middle class blacks, male infidelity may be tolerated if he is taking care of home (i.e. sexual and financial needs are satisfied). Lower income black males may be more tolerant of extramarital sexual activity by their wives. Often, they are more dependent upon their wives for certain services and do not have the economic wherewithal to insure a wife's fidelity. On the other hand, college educated black males are more likely to terminate a marriage if the wife is known to be unfaithful. The norms of his class require him to save face by the rejection of the wandering wife. A lesser educated male may resort to physical abuse to bring the unfaithful wife in line.

However, it is often jealousy, not the act of infidelity, that is a disruptive force in male/female relationships. An act of infidelity is a *fait accompli* and known to both parties. Jealousy is the nagging suspicion that one's partner is unfaithful. It may be based on reality or be a reflection of other psychological forces. At best, it can be an emotionally draining experience for both partners. He may experience anxiety and anger over the feeling that she is consorting with other men. If his suspicions are untrue, she may be pained by his lack of trust in her, the constant accusations and even constraints on her movements and emotions. There are numerous cases of women who eventually were unfaithful in retaliation for the male partner's unfounded suspicions about their fidelity.

While jealousy can be a destructive force in a relationship, there are social forces that have given rise to its increase among married *and* unmarried couples. One of them is the permanent availability of many individuals in American society.[23] Even marriage is no longer seen as a permanent alliance as people constantly exit from relationships in the search for somebody better, the perfect mate. It is common, for instance, for married men who get a divorce to remarry another woman within a year. Often, that woman was a sexual partner during the course of his marriage. While her presence may not have been the dominant factor in the marital disruption, her availability (and pressure) certainly contributed to his willingness to dissolve the marriage. Thus, jealousy that is rooted in the fear of losing one's partner is not totally unfounded.

Another social force impinging on attitudes of jealousy are the changes in the female role. Infidelity was once considered a male practice, with female infidelity subject to all the scorn a society could muster. Various studies indicate that 50–60 percent of wives will engage in extramarital sexual activity during the course of their marriages.[24] In general, women have not engaged in extramarital sex for the same reasons as men — sexual variety and recreation. Often, they were "forced" to do so because of the husband's neglect, sexual incompetency or blatant infidelity. These remain the dominant reasons for infidelity but the sexual revolution and its concomitants have produced a new kind of woman.

We should be clear on what the sexual revolution was all about. It eroded the double sexual standard but did not eliminate all its aspects. Women had been totally denied the pleasures of sex except within the context of marriage. And even today, they still are subject to a different set of standards than men. Men do not expect women to have the same number of sexual partners or variety of sexual experiences as males. And, they are expected to be discrete in the sexual liaisons they do have. At the same time, the legacy of the double standard has provided women with more opportunities for sexual outlets than most men. It is still men who are the buyers and women who are the sellers in the sexual marketplace. For women whose values allow permissive sexual activity, there is no shortage of partners in a sellers' market. Male sexual jealousy may be shaped by this knowledge of a woman's greater chances for sexual adventures. She neither has to wine and dine in order to obtain a sexual consort nor do many men require a commitment from her before indulging in coitus. As one woman remarked: "it's easier to get a man in bed than a drink of water."

Many women have asserted their sexual rights and opportunities. According to one survey, (1) 54 percent of the married women had had extramarital affairs, (2) 55 percent had engaged in sex on their lunch hours, (3) 48 percent had made love with more than one man in the same day, (4) 82 percent had seduced a man at least once. [25] Again, we can see the visible evidence of sexual liberalization among women and the natural concomitant is increased male jealousy. For example, the increase of women in the labor force has brought men and women into contact with each other in heretofore unprecedented ways. A major problem of integrating police cars with male and female officers has been the jealousy of the spouse over such an arrangement. This is especially a problem among white collar workers, where there is ample time for socializing on the job and discretionary time for having sexual affairs.

Another social arrangement that promotes sexual jealousy is the increase in opposite sex friendships. Many of these friendships are platonic and provide an enriching experience in heterosexual communication and interaction. Others are a mask for cheating on one's partner — married or otherwise. Women are more likely to have such friendships since men tend to keep their affairs underground. A woman's male friends are often former lovers who may turn out to be future lovers as well. Some are current lovers masquerading as platonic friends. When one relationship is ended, the woman's next mate is frequently a man who was formerly a "friend." A woman may use a man who is a platonic friend as a reserve lover for the future in case her present relationship does not work out. It is the contact with these men and former lovers that generates much male jealousy.

Women may define boundaries for their male friends that prohibit sexual contact but give the appearance of infidelity. One of the most common examples is permitting male guests to stay overnight in their homes, sometimes sharing the same bed with them. We encountered one woman who could not understand her boyfriend's jealousy. It seems that she told him of her relationship with several men over a period of time. While involved with one man, she allowed another man to pay her air fare to a conference in another city. The man, although married, was a former lover and they slept in the same hotel room without engaging in sex. While at that conference, she invited another man to visit her and stay at her house. By the time of his visit, she was involved with her present boyfriend who objected to the man's visit. The man came anyway and she did not have sexual relations with him. Yet, she had created a low level of trust in her current lover and her continued contact with former lovers did nothing to ameliorate his sexual jealousy.

Coming into contact with former lovers can be a common problem in the black community. Middle class blacks are few in numbers and the places they frequent are the same. Thus, there are numerous cases of black singles dating the friend of a friend. In any social gathering of middle class blacks, an individual's past, present and future lovers may be present. Because this social incest is so pervasive, it may be difficult to maintain a positive image when so much is known about one's sexual affairs. Perforce, indiscreet men may make known their previous sexual affairs with a particular woman, often "passing" her on to their male running partners. Lately, men with lusty sexual appetites have been discussed by their sexual partners and been labeled as "male whores." Women may eschew such a man because "he's been had by everybody." Sleeping around, then, becomes a problem for both sexes. And, it contributes to feelings of sexual jealousy, and social embarrassment, when a mate's previous sexual liaisons are well known.

Women have the greatest cause for sexual jealousy since studies have estimated that as many as 90 percent of American males have had extramarital affairs. While most have no intention of leaving their wives, the "other woman" can be the precipitant force in the termination of a deteriorating marriage.[26] Black women, in particular, face stiff competition for the few available and desirable men. Most of the desirable black males are already married, but some single black women realize that nothing is forever. If unable to find an unattached man, they are not reluctant to seek one who belongs to another woman. As a result, many married black women resign themselves to accepting a man's infidelity, as long as he is not disrespectful. Others adopt the motto, "What's good for the goose is good for the gander." They, too, engage in extramarital affairs although they tend to be more discreet in their sexual liaisons.

The consequences of such a reaction and counter-reaction are predictable. Even in relationships where fidelity is the norm, sexual jealousy may occur. Jealousy may be more a cause of marital disruption than actual infidelity. There is ample evidence that it is a contributory cause to the 130 percent increase in divorces among blacks during the 1970s.[27] Moreover, it has created a low level of trust among blacks engaged in intimate relationships. Single black women are all too aware of the many married men who approach them for dates and sexual favors. Certainly, it is not surprising that many of them see all men as being incapable of having a monogamous marriage. More to the point, they will have a low level of trust in their future husbands, especially if they were married when they embarked on their intimate association.

Sexual jealousy may have always been a reality. But, the current prevalence of infidelity is largely a product of the sexual revolution and the changes in women's roles. In earlier periods, married men were more faithful because there were few women available to them. Women were monogamous because they were economically dependent on men and society punished their sexual transgressions in the harshest manner. A return to the constraints on women is not being argued here. The sexual revolution liberated America from its puritanical and hypocritical moral order and freed the female libido for fuller expression. Still, sexual jealousy is not just a function of negative psychological forces residing in the individual. In many ways it is a realistic reflection of the options people have for sexual variety in their lives and the social arrangements that promote infidelity.

SUMMARY

The problems black men and women have in their relationships often are shaped by external forces. Many have been unable to form a monogamous family due to structural impediments. In a society where money is the measure of the man, many black males are excluded as potential mates because they lack the economic wherewithal to support a family in a reasonable manner. Given the traditional role definitions for women, definitions internalized by many black males, the highly educated black woman finds herself victimized by the fact that she has a higher educational and income level than most of the black men in her pool of eligibles. Both of those factors are products of institutional racism and black history in America. Hence, the conflict between men and women may be more apparent than real. The real problem may be largely a demographic one with strong class overtones. There simply are not enough black men to go around and the ones available are not regarded as viable mates. As Patrice Rushen, the singer, has stated, "I think it is just a way to divert our attention from the fact that we have things that must be done together to make some headway. We're not dealing in times that afford us the luxury of being able to feel there's a problem with black men that automatically creates a problem for the black woman and vice-versa. We have to look for where these problems come from — and we might find it ain't us."28

Regardless of the source of the problem, the high number of unmarried and divorced blacks signals that all is not well between black men and women. The unbalanced ratio of men to women and the greater degree of "power" given to men is a combustible combination that creates a potential problem. In men this power is often manifested as arrogance and insensitivity to women's needs. For women, feelings of insult and injury can add up to outrage. White racism may have been the force which shaped black relationships and its spectre may remain with us for the foreseeable future. However, the future of the black family may rest upon those blacks who resist the notion that racism will determine their personal relationships. Otherwise, it seems clear that racism may have decisively determined the nature of the most intimate association between men and women. Then, their capacity to resist racism itself may be brought into question. A house divided against itself cannot stand.

Chapter Eight

Black Men/White Women

In the mid-Sixties a very controversial book entitled *Sex and Racism in America* was published by Calvin Hernton. The central theme of this book is that the race problem in the United States is inextricably connected with sex. Controversial statements in the book included charges that the white man clearly is obsessed with the idea of blacks desiring sexual relations with whites and black males being secretly tormented with unfulfilled sexual desires for white women.[1]

While Hernton appears to have overstated his case, it is also clear that sexual relations between the races is a subject of much concern to many Americans. A couple of decades ago, the Swedish economist Gunnar Myrdal, while conducting his classical study of American race relations, asked white Southerners to list, by order of importance, the things they thought blacks wanted most. Heading the list was intermarriage and sexual intercourse with whites. When blacks were similarly asked to make the list, inter-marriage and sexual intercourse with whites were ranked last among their desires in life.[2]

Whether the black male wants a white woman or not, it certainly appears that the white male is concerned about preserving the purity of white womanhood. Since 1698 social censure and severe penalties were reserved for the association of black men and white women.[3] The evidence for the white male's obsession is volum-inous, including accusations by lynch mobs that the black man raped or threatened to rape the white woman, the white South's obsession with the purity of white womanhood, the literal castra-

tion of black men for centuries, and the death of a youth like Em-
mett Till, who was killed for looking at a white woman. As Fanon
comments, the white man fears that the black man will "introduce
his daughter into a sexual universe for which the father does not
have the key, the weapons, or the attributes."[4]

BLACK MEN/WHITE WOMEN

The black male/white female dyad has generally been the most
controversial and common interracial duo for the last decade. How
common it is was confirmed by our data.* Approximately 85 percent of the men in our sample had at least one interracial experience. These experiences ranged from a one night fling to marriage. Most liasons began in college, but men who were over 35
years of age or had attended a predominently black school were
more likely to have met their white female partners through work
contacts. A number of men had met their white partners through
political or civil rights activity, others through organizations such
as the Peace Corps and Vista.

In contrast to theories about the inequality of status among biracial couples, almost all the men claimed that the white women
were of equal status. In fact, according to a 39 year old male psy-
chologist, "in terms of family background, most of them were of a
higher status. My father was a janitor. Their fathers were stock-
brokers, medical doctors and wealthy businessmen. I met all of
them in school or through professional activity. They were well-
educated. None of them would be considered poor white trash."

The motivation of black men for dating white women varied
from male to male. Those men still involved in ongoing biracial
dating said they continued in the relationships "for compatibility or
love." Men who had their interracial experiences behind them gave
slightly different responses. A major reason for the initial encounter was the mystique attached to the hitherto unavailable
"white goddess." According to a 36 year old male reporter, "I did it
originally because of the mystique surrounding white women.

---

* The findings in this chapter come from a larger study of 500 college educated
black singles in the United States. Approximately 110 of the sample were black
males. Robert Staples, *The World of Black Singles,* Westport, Connecticut, 1981.
All quotes unless footnoted come from this study.

They were all I ever saw in magazines, books and movies. To me they represented the epitome of beauty and sensuality. The image portrayed was a cure for all my sexual ills as well as a release for all my sexual fantasies. Now I date them because of the same reasons I date any woman — for some sexual gratification, intellectual exchange and to broaden my scope on women of all creeds and color."

Once they had penetrated the mystique of white women (and some men never do) the reasons for dating white females may be very similar to those for dating black women — but they may still be based on the assumption of racial differences in female behavior. Whether it is true or not, one of the presumed differences is that white women are more likely to be sexually permissive. A 29 year old businessman told us: "White women tend to be freer sexually, not only in terms of going to bed faster but in the kind of sexual activity in which they will engage. If you date a black woman you have to beg, plead, cajole and threaten her all night to get a piece of leg. Whereas a white woman will deal with the issue right away — either she will say yes and help you take your clothes off or she'll say no and tell you why. A white woman will go down on you with relish where black women have to be pressured into giving you a blow job. Really, it's just less hassle with a white chick."

While the more liberal sexual behavior of white women vis-a-vis black women is confirmed by our other black male subjects, it is a racial distinction that is not absolute. Unlike the black women they date, white women who date black men are rarely selected at random from the white population. The white women who are available to black men are probably less sexually inhibited than a typical white woman. In part, she is generally more unconventional and liberal than most white women. She is rarely a flag-waving Republican with very conservative social views. And, much of the attraction between black men and white women is sexually based. Neither one of them, in many cases, considers the other as eligible for marriage.

There are black men whose sole experience with white women has been sexual. A 35 year old male teacher reported: "I have balled white women but I've never taken them out to social functions. Usually, they came over to my place and we'd get into a sexual thing. We never went out in public because I didn't have any need, nor could I afford it, to be showboating a white woman." That many white women reciprocate that sentiment is expressed in a quotation by a white woman in *City Magazine:* "It used to be that you could always depend on black men to fuck you and not want to get emotionally involved; in fact you'd only hear from them once every three weeks. But, now they're getting paranoid that white women are ripping them off for their bodies."[5]

THE MOTIVATION

Interracial dating increased around the same time as the advent of the sexual revolution. It was the liberalization of sexual mores, especially for women, that made much of the biracial dating possible. Once sex became divorced from marriage, or the potential for it, white women were able to accept the idea of an interracial sexual liaison without worrying about the social consequences of a biracial marriage. As a result, we find that when women become more oriented toward traditional marriage possibilities, their sexual partners tend to belong to the same racial group. Of course, there are many white women who do not exclude black males as potential husbands. At the same time, as black men grow older the sexual variety becomes less important than finding a stable relationship. Many of them cease their involvement in biracial sexual flings, although others are not racially exclusive in their choice of mates. Moreover, it is becoming evident that the differences in sexual inhibitions between black and white women is narrowing. Hence, there are two tendencies among many black men; women compete for his affection on the basis of factors unrelated to race; or he confines his search for a serious relationship to a homogenous racial pool, in order to avoid the complications of a biracial union.

Another factor in the black male's selection of white women as dating partners is his disenchantment with or dislike for black women. Some of the black men who date white women do so to the total exclusion of black women. They actually stereotype all black women and all white women on the assumption that racial membership *ipso-facto* carries with it negative or positive traits. The negative stereotypes of black women are that they are domineering, sexually inhibited, materialistic and lacking in sophistication.

A number of black women pointed out that the white women involved with black men tended to be ultra-feminine and blond. A few black men gave other reasons for their preference of white women as dating partners. One man, a 29 year old executive said, "Non-black women I find are more friendly, frank, informative and just plain more interesting to be with. The most noticeable thing is that the white and brown women I've dated shared the financial burden of a date more often than not."

One common, and most valid, reason for dating white women is that they are not as likely to expect a commitment from black men or demand one. According to a 33 year old male filmmaker: "Yes, I've dated white women. There seems to be boundless freedom, in terms of the relationships. Black women are okay because you're at home. They are not okay in terms of expectations. They have more of an idea of how and where you fit into their lives and vice-versa. It's a highly defined situation. With white women there is more flexibility in the relationship. If you don't see them one week, they don't complain. They allow you time for your work and other pursuits without getting jealous or demanding."

For many white women an interracial love affair is designed to round out their lives. It is similar to living in Europe for a year in order to enrich one's life and then return home. As a result, some black men report making a marriage proposal to a white woman and having it rejected. Conversely, white women in interracial situations have had the strongest commitment to a serious relationship and experienced rejection at the hands of a black man. One 32 year old male professor informed us: "I've dated two white women. One was my fiancee. On the whole the experience was good. They satisfied most of the expectations of what I desire in a mate. I couldn't marry them because of the racial variables in part and partly because they proved to be too demanding of my affections and attention. And, because of their insecurity. Being white she needed double reassurance of my love — being a white woman and having committed herself to a black man."

MAKING CONTACT

There is no dichotomy between black and white women, interracial and intra-racial unions. The similarities and differences constantly emerge in both groups and situations. Biracial unions continue to be controversial because they contain the same element as race relations in general: the notion of inferior and superior groups. This type of racial stratification is most obviously expressed in the selection of biracial mates. While there are exceptions, most black men do not initiate dating or marital relationships with white women. Only a minority of white women would be receptive to the attempt of a black man to establish an intimate relationship, and be becomes involved only with those white women who, through cues or context, are known to be interested in dating black men. To do otherwise would be to experience rejection of the worst kind. A black female sociologist analyzed this reversal of roles: "The white female does not hold the view that the black male has a cultural right to initiate a relationship with her. . . . In a social order where white beliefs form fundamental explanations of how individuals should enact their color-sex positions and associated role expectations, black males do not, regardless of their economic status or intellectual capabilities, have the cultural prerogative to take the initiative."[6]

Since white women are not available at random, the question is: who are the white women in biracial unions and how do interracial couples meet? Most of our black singles had their initial interracial date in college and met their white partners on the campus where they, too, were students. Although there are no data on the subject, informed observers report a marked decline in biracial dating among black males in the last five years. In part this must be attributed to a more conservative mood on college campuses. The political movements on campus are dormant and there are generally fewer white female students in Black Studies and sociology classes. In addition, few of our black singles are still in school and the place of contact has shifted to the workplace. Moreover, the type of white woman they meet is often different than the one encountered in college. She may be apolitical, although generally liberal, and have little experience with men of other races. In cities such as New York, Washington, Boston and San Francisco there is often a shortage of white males. The white males available may be gay or uninterested in sex. Many single, career-oriented white women find black men more available (to them) and ready for sexual flings.

In certain cities there are known interracial hangouts where white women can be found. Additionally, there appear to be various volunteer associations with heavy concentrations of white women and a few black males. Sometimes, black women, unwittingly, are responsible for introducing a white female into a black setting where she will meet black men. The white woman in question may be a co-worker who is invited to a black affair. The friends and co-workers of white women involved with black men are frequently eligible for a biracial date. A major difference in black/white encounters is that they are not as likely to occur in casual public situations. While white men may meet white women in supermarkets, parks, bars, on tennis courts, while jogging, etc., that option is not as available to black men. This is particularly true in light of recent rape scares. In San Francisco, for instance, 75 percent of the *reported* rape victims are white women and 50 percent of the *arrested* rapists are black males. This makes many white women, even liberal ones, very leery of unsolicited approaches by black men.

THE DIFFERENCE RACE MAKES

Biracial unions are often disrupted for the same reasons as intraracial ones. That, however, does not mean there are no problems in the interracial dyad unrelated to race. Blacks and whites do come from different cultural backgrounds and even similar class status does not eliminate those racial variations. While not a major source of tension, the cultural differences were pointed out by a number of our respondents. A 33 year old male engineer noted: "The experiences have been good. But, you notice the differences in races culturally. You often have to explain the meaning of certain words or customs to them. Musically, their records are not as interesting. The music was good but I didn't feel it deeply. There were cultural differences in the area of cooking, speech, attitudes. The attitude is more visual. It's the different flavors of the same substance. It's not easy to describe." Sometimes these differences can be mutually enhancing in a biracial relationship. The black partner is generally more aware of white culture but may find new and gratifying interests in skiing, classical music, biking and other activities that are not as common in his culture.

Occasionally, there is no cultural interchange. In fact, the white partner may want to deny the significance of race or racism. She may, instead, stress that there are no racial differences and be totally oblivious to the unique character of her biracial relationship. This is not to be unexpected since many whites are not accustomed to thinking in racial terms. Since it is their society they only regard themselves as human, not white. The black partner is accustomed to race being the decisive factor in his life and is very sensitive to race-related behavior. A 35 year old male artist commented: "One of the problems with whites is their lack of knowledge of what it is like to be rejected for something over which you have no control. You run into whites who feel they can take liberties — like asking racially oriented questions or making puns — not thinking that it would be a sensitive area. They don't recognize discrimination when it appears — like having to wait a long time in a restaurant before being served."

In contradistinction to the white women who deny the existence of race are those women who take on all the elements of black culture, including the sensitivity to racism. These women literally give up their white identity for a black one. A 39 year old male educator reported: "I met this one white woman at a black place and didn't know at first she was white. There seemed to be no racial differences because she had been around blacks all her life. She dated mostly black men. In fact, I find most of the white women whom I have dated have dated blacks before and they have become black also." While imitation may be the highest form of flattery, there are some black men who avoid black-acting white women. They may do so because they believe such imitation has a false ring to it or is a reflection of the white woman's need to negate her own racial identity. Although some white women may take on elements of black culture, speech, clothes, and hairstyles, others date black males exclusively when their former interracial affair has produced a child who is labeled black by society. Some white women date black men exclusively because they prefer the style of black men and consider their sexual prowess better than that of white men.

The problems in biracial unions may only differ in kind from those faced by same-race couples or not be serious enough to cause the disruption of a relationship. A more serious problem, and the major one, is the external pressure on the biracial couple. Those pressures come primarily from two groups of people who are opposed to any mixing of the races; namely, black women and white men. The women resent the loss of one of their men and the implication that white women are superior to them; white men resent the alleged degradation of white womanhood. The opposition of white men to black men / white women liaisons is generally acknowledged and has been expressed, historically, in their violent acts against black men who crossed the color line. While the opposition remains strong among them, interracial couples rarely face the violent intimidation of the past in most large cities of America.

Nowadays, white antipathy toward biracial couples is expressed in more subtle ways such as stares, whispers and avoidance of close contact with them. This is generally true only in large cities. If biracial couples were to venture into what is called redneck territory, they would encounter some difficulty. A 38 year old government employee told us of being attacked by a group of white men after he was observed camping with a white woman in a rural area of California. The recent emergence of the white backlash has generated more open opposition to interracial couples among many whites. A black male newspaper reporter, age 44, commented:

> You'd be surpised how many people around Westwood are openly beginning to say nasty things about interracial couples. During the 1960's, nobody cared about interracial situations. There seemed to be a greater feeling of liberalism and change like we were really on the verge of a new world or something. Not today, however. Maybe it's the economy but I've heard more students telling nigger jokes and white girls who date black guys being called Beulah by their friends. Maybe it's the competition for jobs, but 10 years ago it sure wasn't like that.

THE OPPOSITION

Some of the opposition by white males to black male/white female alliances may be their fear of black sexual competition and the cultural stereotype of black males as superior lovers. One study demonstrated that even liberal white males harbor strong resentments against the black male/white female dyad.[7] Knowledge of these attitudes led a 35 year old male social scientist to conclude:

"I've dated many white women and some of them have been really good people. Yet, I've always remained uncommitted for a possible permanent relationship. There's just too much race conflict. The Bakke case and anti-busing demonstrations are only the tip of the iceberg. I have a hunch that black people are in for some rough times ahead. And, I'd rather weather that storm with a sister that I know understands and is affected in the same way by those problems."

Racial conflict would mean increased stresses in the future for biracial couples. In the here and now, a more troublesome source of tension is the often outraged opposition of black women. In contrast, some whites have looked very favorably upon blacks involved in biracial unions because they perceive them to be less hostile to whites in general. Black women, however, are greatly disturbed by black male/white female affairs for understandable, if greatly exaggerated, reasons. While white women have been blamed for every ill that plagues the black community, the main charge against them is that they have taken away some of the most prestigious black men from black women. A 34 year old female nurse comments: "Being a black single woman is difficult. There are just not enough eligible men. Those who are available have not gotten over the white woman syndrome. The white woman has the best of both worlds: she has white and black men. Anytime she wants to, she can return home to the white man. And, the black man will just seek out another white woman. I don't like being alone but it looks like I have no other choice."

What bothers many black women is their belief that they simply cannot compete with white women for black men, because almost any white woman fits the dominent society's standard of beauty better than most black women, the white woman has an inherent advantage over black women. A common charge by black women is that the white woman in biracial unions is physically unattractive. According to a 39 year old female account executive: "You just want to scream when you see a white woman, who is no way your equal, marching off with a handsome, bright black man. You know the relationship is based on her whiteness. He would never accept a black woman who looked like that." Whereas there may be some validity to this point of view, it is possible to explain the attraction in other ways. Black men select from the white women available to them and among that group will be few truly beautiful women because they do not exist in great abundance among the white population. Very attractive white women are often able to bargain for a white mate with a much higher status than most black men are able to achieve. On the other hand, the most attractive black women are available to those black men who hold high status in their culture. However, the white women in interracial relationships represent a variety of physical types.

Regardless, black women feel especially pained at what they perceive to be the black male's rejection of them in favor of white women. And, they have expressed their resentment in very explicit ways. One black male, a 32 year old architect, reported: "At my college there were a few black girls dating white guys but mostly black dudes with white girls. This really made black girls jealous. It was not uncommon for the black guy to find "honkey lover" written on his car. One time a bunch of sisters cornered a white girl who was dating a brother in the ladies room and cut off all her hair. The black males on campus got along pretty well with the white students but many of the girls believed in black separatism and acted very hostile toward whites."

THE COSTS

There are penalties imposed on black men publicly associated with white women. A number of black leaders and scholars often have their accomplishments and their biracial liaisons spoken of in the same breath, so strong is the consciousness of them as men consorting outside the race. One black male who heads a black-oriented organization told us: "I liked the white women I was involed with but stopped because of the political consequences. White women aren't as persistent about getting a commitment as black women. But, black women fit in better with my business interests." A number of prominent black men we interviewed asked us not to reveal that they dated white women. As a 34 year old female sales representative declared: "When I meet a black male who I feel is strong, and has demonstrated by his actions, a concern for our struggle and I find he has a white wife, it still invalidates his achievements for me."

Such vehement responses by black women force many black men to be circumspect in their interracial affairs. While a few black males have enough audacity to bring a white date to a predominantly black affair, most eschew such visibility. As a 28 year old male businessman said: "In dating white women I would avoid any large gathering of blacks. I would rather be exposed to more whites than blacks. I wouldn't want to be singled out among blacks as 'the brother with the white woman.' Places that we'd go or things we'd do would be out of the ordinary. We'd go to the woods or the forest." Having to cut off ties with the black community can create problems for the black male and his white partner. According to a 32 year old male writer: "The white relationships were okay but they increased my sense of isolation from black people. The social pressures were too difficult to contend with. I'd disappear on weekends. I'd spend them at parties. I wouldn't take her. I even gave some and didn't invite her. The social pressures made me feel guilty. It's more difficult today than 10 years ago."

As a result of these pressures some black men have to alter their lifestyles to accommodate their biracial relationship. In cities such as New York, Boston, Berkeley and San Francisco there are enough liberal white circles in which to circulate. However, this is not a viable option for some black men. One, a 30 year old lawyer, told us: "While I've never been relaxed in all-white situations, maybe because I was from the South, going out with white people was the only safe thing to do. I did not like to be seen in public. I was paranoid. In private I could deal with it." Another recourse was to join the network of other interracial couples. A few black males reported that most of their associates were other biracial couples. Mostly, these black/white couples were composed of black men/white women. Although a number of our black males claim to have many white female friends and intimates, few of them regarded any white males as close friends.

Not all the opposition to biracial dating comes from black women and white men. A few black males have joined in the crusade. Nathan Hare, a prominent black sociologist, has stated that white women were introduced into the black community to cause a rift between black men and women, hence disrupting the black struggle for liberation.[8] Another prominent black male social scientist has declared in an unpublished paper that all black men dating or married to white women, should be expelled from the "community." The overwhelming majority of the black men in our study have engaged, or are presently involved, in an interracial relationship. Those who were not or had not, cited as their reason a basic mistrust of all whites. One such man, a 38 year old college professor asserted: "It's hard to tell if white women are genuine and whether or not to trust them. I don't believe that white women can give up whiteness for a human relationship."

For many of our black men, interracial dating was a time-contained, and basically pleasant, experience. There were many of them who claimed the primary motivation for their action was the unavailability of black women. This would be true for the black men who attended predominantly white colleges prior to 1968. Most of those schools had extremely small black enrollments (typically less than 20 blacks) and the majority of them were black males, primarily athletes. As a result of penetrating the mystique surrounding white women, some found the interracial affair a pleasant one and continued such associations well into their post college lives, and a few up to the present. In other cases, they may have ceased all interracial dating because of the social pressures. Those involved in biracial dating because of antipathy for black women or who ceased such activities due to an antipathy toward white women are guilty of racial stereotyping. The positive and negative attributes of women in general can be found in both races. The real problem is that, in the present context, biracial dating and marriage contains stone and mortar for the building of walls between people, sexes and races alike.

SUMMARY

Interracial mating is a subject fraught with controversy. Those who oppose it often combine a hostility toward institutional racism with invidious assessments of the private thoughts and lives of interracial couples. Many black men and white women mate for no more complex reasons than meeting, liking each other as individuals and choosing to transcend the societal barriers to their relationship. Only in societies similar to the one in the United States does a biracial union take on any greater significance. For centuries, Latin American nations have undergone such a fusion of the races that only nationality, language and religion remain as sources of identity.[9] But the painful history of race relations in North America militates against the natural mixing of individuals from different races. Instead of adopting the philosophy that individuals who choose to date and marry is a matter of personal choice, many blacks have taken up the call for racial purity so common to their white supremacy adversaries of the past.

Despite the opposition to biracial unions, they will continue to increase, among both men and women, as long as the social forces that set miscegenation into motion are extant. There is, for example, the class factor. As long as middle class blacks occupy token positions in the upper reaches of the job hierarchy, most of the people they meet in their occupational world will be white. Considering the fact that the job setting is the paramount place for meeting mates, it is only natural that many blacks will date and marry whites. Those whites will be the people they most often encounter and with whom they share common values, interests and lifestyles. Almost 25 years ago, E. Franklin Frazier predicted:

> The increasing mobility of both white and colored peoples will not only provide a first-hand knowledge of each for the other but will encourage a certain cosmopolitanism. That means there will be a growing number of marginal people who will break away from their cultural roots. These marginal people will help create not only an international community but an international society. In becoming free from their local attachments and provincial outlook, they will lose at the same time their racial prejudices, which were a product of their isolation. Many of these marginal people will form interracial marriages because they are more likely to find suitable marriage partners in the cosmopolitan circles than within their native countries.[10]

Not all blacks who consort with non-blacks will do so for noble motives. Becauses blacks tend to stereotype each other in negative terms, many will cross the color line to find what they believe is "absent" in their own race. However, many of the alleged advantages of the white female actually result from her longer tenure and security in her class position. It is easier, for instance, to enact the traditional female role when the men in your class — and race — can fulfill the normative masculine role and few black males have been allowed that opportunity in a racially stratified society.

Even more important is the fact that crossing racial lines does not eliminate the normal stresses and tensions that occur between men and women. The 78 percent increase of the divorce rate for whites during the past decade obviously indicates that they are encountering their share of problems with each other. Add to that the fact that *intra*racial marriages have a considerably lower dissolution rate, it is clear that marrying across racial lines is no quick solution to the intractable problems of male/female conflict.[11]

The wave of the future, however, does not seem to be the black male/white female dyad. Increasingly, black women are dating and marrying white males. The attention of society in general and black women, in particular has focused on black men and white women, and has overlooked the fact that the most common interracial pairing in the sixties were black women and white men. Some studies reveal that as many as 49 percent of black women have dated white men.[12] As black women ascend in the middle class world, they, too, will mate on the basis of proximity and class interests. Previously, fewer black women engaged in interracial mating because white males were not interested in them, at least not for marriage. As racial barriers drop in the society in general, especially among the middle classes, the opportunity structure will increase for black women, and the outcome will be the same for them as for black men. Whether their biracial unions will be any more durable may depend primarily on the trajectory of social forces in the society at large.

Part V:
Masculinity and Sexism

CHAPTER NINE:

Black Manhood in the 1970's: A Critical Look Back

At the end of the sixties a new era was ushered in for black men. The seventies witnessed the bourgeoning of black nationalism with its attendant elevation of the black male to his "rightful" and historical role as head of the black family and community. Instead, the seventies proved to be a decade where women, mostly white, a few black, gained ascendency. As it was, the decade's flowering of black manhood turned into a withering away of what little supremacy they had and consigned many black men into a prison of their gender. While the changes that occurred in the seventies had an impact on all black people, since it is an indivisible group, there are forces that differently affect the male segment. The dominant force is the masculine mystique that infects black men and its interface with institutional racism.

Institutional racism and its machinations shape the expression of black masculinity. Yet, it is incumbent upon us to examine our notions of manhood and how that subjective definition fits into the objective consequences that black men encounter in American society. As with most aspects of human behavior, it begins with the socialization process. If we consider the male children of today, a majority will be raised in female headed households. The reasons for the father's absence range from the existence of welfare regulations that force the father out of the home, a man's inability to secure gainful employment to support his family, tensions in the male/female relationship, and the fact that a majority of black children are born out of wedlock. This latter reason represents one of the most basic contradictions of black masculinity. It is the urge

135

to prove one's manhood through sexual adventures and the society's barriers to fulfillment of the masculine ideal. The young black male proves his manhood by siring a child but American society denies him the economic resources to support that child.

Perforce, most of our male children are raised by their mothers in today's society. We have been told that such children cannot adequately learn to be men. Alas, that is not the problem. They learn to be men all too well. Their mothers socialize them well into the masculine role as do surrogate male role models in their midst. Not only do their mothers train them for a masculine ideal but they provide them with a deference that they come to expect in later life. In other words, they are all too often given a mother's unmitigated love but denied a father's firm discipline and unquestioned authority. The result is too many men who fail to take on the responsibility that manhood entails.

Let us be clear that blame for the alleged failures of black men is not being shifted to the women who raise them. There is culpability enough in all sectors of the society. Unraveling the complexities of how black men came to be what they are is not a simple task, suffice it to say that their gender seems to be the decisive factor. Black women have more than their share of problems. Those problems, while no less serious for them, have a different configuration. It is the men that we see wandering aimlessly along the streets of city ghettoes, narcotized by drugs or alcohol. They are the ones who resort to acts of self-destruction, in unprecedented numbers, of homocide, suicide and street crime. Even when they are successful in American terms, something plagues them about their masculinity. It is what I call the masculine mystique and it appears to be worth examining.

YOUNG MACHO AND THE SUCCESS MYTH

How can we account for the fact that black male children consistently perform below grade level at a rate twice as high as black females in the public schools? In the predominantly black school system of Oakland, California, special classes to prepare students for careers in science and business are populated mostly by females. Even when black males sit in a classroom for twelve years and graduate from high school, they are less likely to read and write well than any other group (except Latino males) in this country. At present, there are a hundred thousand more black women enrolled in college than black men. Probably, double that number will actually graduate and receive a degree. These gender differences transcend class lines as even middle class black male children are not faring as well in public and private schools as their sisters.

The conventional wisdom would have us blame the school system for what happens to black male children in their custody. Still, is it only a conspiracy against black males? I think not. Certainly, the schools must bear their share of responsibility for the miseducation of black children. Yet in the case of black males, a peer oriented system serves to divert many of them into the pursuit of show business and athletic careers. While there are historical reasons for blacks centering on entertainment and sports, when there were few other options open to them, the circumstances of black career mobility have changed. But, it is primarily the females whose activities are guided by those changes. As Harry Edwards has noted, "Second class citizenship renders Black male youths highly vulnerable to the pull factor of a 'manhood hustle' in both sport and the military."[1]

A situation exists where black female youths are preparing for careers in science, medicine, business and education while the young men aspire to be the nation's jocks and soldiers. Edwards also comments that "perhaps three million black youths between 13 and 22 are dreaming of careers as professional athletes. But, the odds against them are at least 20,000 to 1."[2] Ironically, it is in the field of sports that the masculine ideal is most frequently violated. Both professional and amateur athletes work under the constant supervision and vigilance of white coaches. They have much less autonomy in their personal and professional lives than blacks in other occupations. It has been only in recent years that black athletes have dared speak out against racism or break the strictures on when they go to bed, have sex, who they marry and other constraints placed on them. And, there is plenty of racism in sports against which to rebel.

One very honest owner of a basketball team was quoted as admitting to maintaining a racial quota on his team, explaining "White people have to have White heroes. I myself can't equate to

Black heroes. I'll be truthful. I respect them, but I need White people. It's in me."³ After a career that lasts less than five years, the
black athlete is stripped further of his dignity. Only 10 percent of
those who go to college actually graduate. As Lou Brock, a retired
baseball star, comments: "There are very few places in this game
for a Black guy when he retires. He's not moved into the front
office. He's not moved into a managerial position. He's not made a
scout, no matter what he's accomplished, no matter what he
knows."⁴

Perhaps it's a bit simplistic to attribute the black male's preoccupation with sports as a major factor in his educational failures.
Certainly, other forces contribute to the problem. Among his male
peers, demonstrating his masculine prowess in terms of sexual conquests, athletic success or fighting is all that is rewarded. The male
who studies and works hard is a pariah among his male cohorts.
Young women, on the other hand, remain more under the control
of their family. Other than becoming pregnant by a young macho,
their conformity fits into the schooling techniques much better and
they succeed. The lack of discipline in the public schools has also
worked against the interests of black male students. It has led to a
veritable epidemic of violence, drugs and absenteeism in the pubilc
schools. The greatest advantage of many private schools is that
they do impose discipline and standards on *all* their students. Even
middle class black parents have taken their children out of the
public schools. Consequently, we have a two-tiered educational
system: one where students get a diploma, another where they get
an education.

Those who receive a diploma but no visible skills will wind up in
one of two avenues of life. Many will be unemployed because as
Jencks concluded "For Blacks, finishing high school only counts
for almost nothing."⁵ Certainly, the unemployment statistics for
young black men confirm the futility of a high school education.
Only a fourth of them have regular and good paying jobs. Apart
from the problem of having few skills, an inability to read and write
well and poor work habits, black teenagers have a much poorer
network of job contacts than whites.⁶ Whites are able to obtain jobs
through a network of friends and relatives that is simply unavailable to most blacks. As many as two thirds of all initial jobs are ob-

tained in this manner.[7] Conversely, black female youths can secure employment in the ever increasing field of clerical work. While the number of jobs available to men with a strong back and little else has been shrinking, the white collar jobs designed for women have undergone a great expansion. Some white males have seen the light and joined women behind a typewriter. Black men refuse to compromise their masculinity by indulging in "feminine work."

Only one other avenue is open to most of them. Again, Edwards has concluded that "it is the manhood appeal that often provides inducement for Black parents to sign their sons into the military — the understanding being that, like sports participation the military experience 'makes men' out of them."[8] Presently, the volunteer army is one-third black, compared with only 12 percent in the general population. As true of society at large, most of them are at the lower rungs. Only 7 percent of the officers are black.[9] While the armed services have been touted as a paragon of equal opportunity and race relations, all is not well in the military area. Recently, there has been a dramatic increase in Ku Klux Klan activity among off-duty servicemen. Observers report some Klan activity aboard naval ships and at European bases. These reports notwithstanding, it is black servicemen who are being sent to army prisons. While they make up less than one third of the army ranks, they account for more than 51 percent of the prison population. Most can not avail themselves of black legal representation, since only 4 percent of the army's lawyers are black.[10] Of course, these statistics only mirror the reality of civilian society.

The "manhood hustle" channels black males into the army because they have no viable options in civilian society. Few, however, recognize any tangible enrichment of their manhood after the military experience. After all is said and done, the military is about killing and dying. Wanting to prove their manhood contributes toward black males joining the more dangerous elite military units (such as the paratroopers and special forces) in far greater proportion than their numbers in the regular army. In the Vietnam war, for instance, 26 percent of all casualties were black. The aftershocks of that war were even more devastating for the blacks who served in it. Even with the high rate of drug addiction, unemployment, crime and psychological problems of black male civilians, the Vietnam war veterans have an even higher rate.[11] It is a terribly high price to pay for one's manhood.

Those who cannot get into the armed services have little left but a life of street crime. While crime is obviously a function of poverty and racism, it is also — we must repeat — a function of gender. Black women are often in equally dire economic straits but continue to represent less than 5 percent of all black criminals. Of course, those with children can avail themselves of welfare support. Still, it is the street wise male-oriented system that channels many black men into crime. Many start off in gangs specializing in petty theft and graduate to large scale robberies. A large number of black criminal acts are committed in tandem and represent the buddy system. The violence accompanying those acts are another reflection of black macho. And, it is partially the violence, representing a threat to personal safety, that causes society to punish street criminals more harshly than white collar criminals.

Black macho notwithstanding, the rate of criminal arrests and convictions are a reflection of class inequalities in the United States. Although white collar crime is estimated to cost the society over 100 billion dollars a year compared to 2.5 billion dollars annual loss from street crimes, the prisons are occupied primarily by lower income and third world males. Whites, for instance, are jailed at a rate of 43.5 per 100,000 while black prisoners number 367.5 per 100,000. The sentences of blacks average 20 percent longer than whites.[12] During the seventies the unemployment rate for blacks increased dramatically as did their percentage of the prison population. In the state of California the minority prison population increased from the 1970 rate of 30 percent to 60 percent in 1979.[13] It is not that whites are not arrested for crimes; they just are not sent to prison as often. The racial violence in that state's prisons has been intensified to such an extent that judges apparently will send only the most incorrigible white man to prison. Imprisonment only strengthens the masculine mystique. A man who does not fit the masculine ideal is soon wasted under the brutal conditions of prison life.

MEN IN THE ECONOMY

If black men should survive the youthful years, fulfilling the masculine ideal is not an easy task. It is at this point that the advantage of the masculine role becomes questionable. Certain social forces have undermined whatever advantages black men had *qua* men. Foremost among them were changes in the economy and the women's liberation movement. Whether it was due to inflationary pressures that propelled women into the labor force or a feminist ideology, the fact remains that of all new employees entering private industry, between 1974 and 1977, 53 percent were white women, 26 percent were white men, 5 percent were black women and black men experienced no net gain in their numbers.[14] Indeed, nearly 40 percent of black men are no longer in the labor force. The estimates of black unemployment by the National Urban League, based on their survey of black households, is placed at one out of every four households. While the low income uneducated black male is the first to drop out of the labor force, his middle class brothers have not fared much better. More dependent on affirmative action policies, he has found himself replaced by the latest "minority" — white women.[15]

There is a general consensus — supported by statistical data — that corporate affirmative action programs have been far more productive for white women than for black men. According to Bernard Anderson, an economist, "employers see White women as substitutes for Black labor, and, especially in periods of slow economic growth, this results in decreased labor market opportunities for Blacks."[16] To a certain extent, black women categorized as "twofers" (i.e. black and female) have made some job advancements because they are counted twice on government compliance reports. But,they are being employed and advanced less rapidly than white women albeit faster than black men. A few candid white male employers admit that they devote more attention and effort to recruiting and training women and far less to advancing black men.

Few women — black or white — have rallied to the defense of black men being excluded from affirmative action programs. In fact, the Minneapolis-Saint Paul Chapter of the National Organization for Women (NOW) issued a report that "disadvantages due to sex are greater than those due to race" and concluded that "current affirmative action efforts are directed disproportionately toward racial minorities."[17] Off the record, white male employers complain that black men are arrogant, impatient and unwilling to conform to business standards. Translated, that means that many black males rebelled against the token and powerless character of the positions they were given. Again, the masculine mystique reasserts itself and the more pliable female — black and white — is seen as less of a threat and her entry into the job arena is facilitated. Of course, the real enemy in this scenario is the government and big employers who keep both blacks and women either out of work or in low paying job categories.

Not all black men have performed admirably in their new found positions. Some were enticed by the illusions of power — something they rarely possessed. Yet, they have convinced themselves — and others — that they could perform certain acts which were not within their purview. This has been particularly acute in Washington, D.C., a city run on power politics. Among black men, it has been an arrogance of powerlessness that has led them into gigantic ego trips. In their wake, they have left trails of unfulfilled promises to blacks who believed in them. Even worse, some have taken on the trappings of their white peers in the executive suites. Increasingly, cases of sexual harassment of female employees are coming to public attention. Black women are often the victims and black men the culpable parties. Some black men, who have not indulged in economic rape, find themselves too preoccupied with proving their sexual prowess to devote much effort to the mastery of their jobs.

To unemployed black men, such practices are beyond the pale. While we realize the economic consequences of unemployment, the psychological ramifications can be more malevolent. In a society where work and money is the measure of the man, joblessness can destroy the male's motivation to live. Because of the masculine mystique, losing a job can cause damage to the fragile male ego, result in suicide, homocide, psychological breakdown and family violence. It is no wonder that many black families are torn asunder by the male's unemployment. Instead of allowing his wife to pick up the slack and pitching in with domestic chores, he often resorts to abusive behavior toward his wife and children or engages in extramarital affairs, all to bolster his deflated ego or re-assert his masculinity.

THE MASCULINE MYSTIQUE

Men who fall victim to the masculine mystique often pay a high penalty. The low life expectancy of black males is known but the cause of it is not merely their greater susceptibility to illness. In this society men have a lower life expectancy than women and black men have the lowest life expectancy of all groups (except Native Americans). The sex differential is greater for black men and women. One reason is that the black woman is more likely to visit a doctor and receive the treatment that is prescribed. The masculine mystique indoctrinates men into ignoring an illness until it becomes disabling; often they do not follow prescribed treatments. When one considers the high mortality rate among young black men (20– 35 years), it is obviously the operative effects of the masculine mystique. With homocide, accidents and suicide ranked as the three leading causes of death, it seems that proving one's manhood can be deadly as well as costly.

The masculine mystique we have been discussing has not always been an integral element of the male image in black culture. In the 1970s that image began to change due to the shift in socialization from the family to the mass media. The image conveyed of black men on television can best be characterized as irresponsible, hypersexualized, hustlers and violent. Rarely has a black man been presented as sensitive, honest, insightful and intelligent. Those images were very real to impressionable black youths, who had no other role models in their environment. Unlike the past, where there was a class mix in the black community, the middle class has fled to the suburbs, taking with them the legitimate role models needed by black youths. So, it was the prototype of the guileful, often violent, hustler that remained for them to draw upon for an image of black manhood. Moreover, the same mass media presented to him an image of the good life and the accouterments that were its concomitants. Unlike many white youths, he did not have parents who could provide him with the commodities so abundantly visible in the media world. What this led to was an individualism and materialism that had been heretofore alien to the black community. And, it was fueled by the masculine mystique which defined his manhood in terms of those possessions.

In its incipient stage, the materialism and individualism of black youths are generated by feelings of alienation, cynicism and hopelessness, feelings that are also common among white youths. When *Newsweek* magazine surveyed blacks in 1979, approximately 40 percent expressed the belief that they are taken advantage of, the people running the country don't care about them, they feel hopeless about their chances to make it and are justified in ripping off whatever they can get.[18] While their analysis of this society and their life chances may be accurate, the ensuing opportunism has its most salient implications for the black community. Few whites are the victims of their predatory behavior. As Poussaint has noted: "I think a lot of drug abuse and alcoholism is part of narcissism, focus on self. I also think it plays a role in crime, like homocide, where the kinship bonds with other people in the community are so weak, and an individual is so concerned with his own needs, that he's ready to kill to save face, or to save his own ego. They don't care enough about the impact of their behavior on other people, and what their own contribution should be to society."[19]

It is, perhaps, reasonable to ask about the role of black leadership in this situation. A predominantly male leadership is in wide disrepute today. The leaders of the past, whose authority to lead resided in their charisma and ideology, were systematically wiped out by the ruling class. Those left, claims Grace Boggs, took advantage of the threat to the social order which black youths posed to demand and get administrative jobs for themselves in schools and other public institutions.[20] The black leaders of today were installed by the media and ruling class. Their leadership is based on a pragmatic adaptation to white institutions and values. Moreover, they suffer from the same delusions of grandeur as do their brothers in the corporate world. Black mayors have gained control of cities with a declining population and tax base at precisely the time the power to deliver jobs, money, education and basic services is shifting to the private sector. Thus, their quest for public office often amounts to no more than male ego aggrandizement.

Their ascendency to public office seems to be part and parcel of a neocolonial strategy. Although black nationalists led the struggle for black liberation in Newark and Oakland, the reins of city hall were taken by an engineer and a former judge. These men are chained to a system that has as its main goals the protection of profits for the corporate world and a safe haven for the middle class during daytime hours. However, their value to the ruling class if diminishing as their credibility continues to decline in the black community. More and more, the black masses demonstrate their discontent with contemporary black leadership by failing to vote, by small scale rebellions in Miami and Philadelphia and critical statements. A black journalist who traveled the South incognito reported that "one of the strongest messages I got from the people I met on the road was that Black elected officials had better look out. An accountability is coming that will be a crisis for many of them."[21]

Turning to a black female leadership might do little to improve the situation of blacks if women, too, become wedded to the same values and institutions. Within the system, however, women do tend to be true believers in their goals. Unlike many men, they try to make improvements in the conditions of lower income blacks. Although there are few black women in high public office, it is noticeable that they have rarely been accused of the misuse of political office and funds that are common to their male counterparts. It would appear that their quest for public office is more motivated by a sincere desire to serve the people than the male's aspirations for the perquisites of political power and the ego elevation that entails.

SUMMARY

It is in the area of interpersonal relationships that the masculine mystique of the seventies has had its greatest impact. Prior to the seventies, especially in the South, a man's status was based on being a stable husband and father. His masculinity was complemented by having a wife, protecting and treating her well. While that aspect of the masculine role remains for many black men, others have taken their gender guide from movie and television depictions of black men. They have taken on a role model that can be characterized as the carefree, hustling superstud caricature.

It is what we call the pimp syndrome where women are viewed as objects of exploitation — sexual and economic. Such an attitude has flourished in an environment where women outnumber men by a ratio of 2-1. This is more than male chauvinism — it is capitalism on the make. And, it has left us with a community where women are forced to work and raise children alone. Only a minority of black women are presently married and living with their spouses.[22]

All this cannot be said without acknowledging that institutional racism and capitalism provided the framework in which male attitudes and behavior are operationalized. But, it is simplistic and self-serving for black men to attribute all that they do to the system. It denies their ability to have free will and to resist forces that are inimical to the black community. Moreover, this narcissism, materialism and opportunism are creatures of the 1970s, features of American life in general. Prior to 1970, even when the black community was buffeted by a caste system which ordered its life chances, there was a notion of masculinity that was respectful of the rights of others. Perhaps the worst tragedy of all is that black men have been victimized the most by the new masculine mystique. The forces that militate against them were set into motion by larger societal institutions. Unfortunately, they have proven to be a willing accomplice to their own destruction.

CHAPTER TEN:

Black Macho
vs. Black Feminism

The modern women's movement is barely ten years old. In that decade it was largely populated by middle class white women who focused on symbolic and class-bound issues, such as protesting against the use of women as sex objects in magazines and attempting to put more women into corporate boardrooms and other male domains. By and large, black women were not present, in large numbers, in the mainstream women's movement, a conspicuous absence since many white women took them as models of strong, independent women, though black women such as Aileen Hernandez, Flo Kennedy, et al., were leading spokeswomen for women's issues. It was said that black women were already liberated, that white women were as racist as white men and that the middle class issues on which the movement focused were irrelevant to the largely working class black population.

Moreover, until recently the black male has been spared as a target of feminists. Afterall, he was certainly in no position to be a sexist, whether he wanted to be or not. White feminists generally left him alone in their assault on men. Many were careful to refer to white male domination as their main gripe. In the last few years, however, a few of them adopted a more strident approach. Black males can now be attacked, not as the banker denying white women credit, but as the sadistic rapist lurking in the alley to terrorize and sodomize them. Although mostly black women were raped, white women were screaming rape.[1] This almost seemed a throwback to the fifties and before when the worst crime possible was the violation of a white woman's body. To rape black women

was tolerable; to sexually assault a white women was an abomina-
tion and a sign of not knowing one's place. This is the gist of the
matter as revealed in the works of Susan Brownmiller[2] and Diana
Russell.[3]

In this era of racist retrenchment it would not be appropriate for
white women to come down too hard on black men. Afterall, white
women had meticulously set themselves apart from white men only
a few years ago when they were labelled "minorities" and placed into the affirmative action pool with Afro-Americans, Asians,
Latinos and Native Americans. Some have called this a cynical
manipulation of the symbols of minority status. At best it served to
defuse the movement of other minorities and to decrease their
chances of upward mobility. Since white feminists could not mar-
shall an all-out attack on black males, and well-known black female
activists such as Joyce Ladner and Angela Davis would not, a few
black feminists took up the pen as a sword, among them Ntozake
Shange[4] and Michele Wallace.[5]

It is strange that this attack on black men should occur when
black women threaten to overtake them, in terms of education, occupation and income by the next century. True, lower class black
women are not faring well, but lower class black men are in even
worse condition. Perhaps one factor in the rise of feminism among
middle class black women is the lack of suitable male partners:
There are 118 college educated black women to every 100 similar
black males; the interracial marriage rate increased by one third in
the seventies and 54 percent of all adult black women never marry,
or are separated, widowed or divorced.[6]

BLACK MALE SEXISM

What obscures the issue at hand here is the lack of a reasonable
and articulate male point of view. Those things that bother black
men — feelings of inferiority, fear of vulnerability — are not often
talked about. What is articulated comes out sounding like insensi-
tive male chauvinism: accusing black women of being domineering, sexually hungup and the like. Little wonder that workshops on
black relationships sometimes degenerate into shouting matches.

On the other hand, black women have begun to link their
grievances to the feminist cause. Some feminists, for example,

seem to be angriest at black men who date and marry white women, and at the poverty of black women. Whether one is for or against miscegenation, and I am indifferent, it would appear to be a matter of personal choice. Certainly, it seems a strange choice of subject to link to the feminist cause. As far as the poverty of black women is concerned, there is little that black men have to do with that and even less that they can do to improve the condition. Of course, most people would agree that men should help to support, even raise, children that they sire — within the extent of their ability to do so. Again, that is a matter between the father and mother, or the courts as a last resort. It does not seem to be a strong issue among white feminists.

Some black feminists have charged that black men deny women meaningful positions in civil rights organizations. It would be more objective to place the issue in a historical context. During the sixties there was a general consensus — among men and women — that black men would hold the leadership positions in the movement. The reasoning behind this philosophy was that black women had held up their men for too long and it was time for the men to take charge. That some black men used the movement to their exclusive advantage cannot be denied. Again, the rationale was based on the "trickle-down" theory: that by enabling black men to advance, the entire black family would be uplifted, and the majority of the black men in the movement pursued a more decent and humane existence for all black people.

If we choose to view gender roles and behavior, that was traditional and normative ten years ago, as sexist today, then all black black men stand guilty of retroactive male chauvinism. The fact that male behavior was normative behavior until recently redefined as sexism poses some theoretical problems for feminists. Unlike other minorities who suffered physically at the hands of their oppressors, women were generally a protected group who were revered by men and children alike. Obviously they were limited in their intellectual and creative expression, but society operated on a *quid pro quo* basis. Many men never liked the idea of having to work to support a family either. Yet, society never held out any other option for them nor any exemption from fighting America's wars or doing its dirty work. Black women, of course, did not share in the privileges of white women and neither did black men partake of the dominant power of white men. The issue here is that what is often defined as sexist behavior is nothing more than men acting in ways in which they have been socialized to act. That they continue to act this way, in the face of warnings from feminists, signals that life-long socialization is not easily reversed; many women cater to and prefer traditional male behavior and no group gives up its privileges without a prolonged struggle.

Still, the problem of defining what is sexist behavior among black men is a complicated one. On the institutional level, most black men do not have the power to force women into subordinate roles. Most of the institutions in which black people are located are controlled by whites. The most significant exception, the black church, has a male leadership and a largely female constituency. However, it is difficult to make a case for black male sexism in the church, simply because most black men are not in the church. That only leaves one other black-controlled institution in which sexism can manifest itself: the family and there is considerable disagreement over how much power black men have in the family, since they are almost as absent from the family as they are from the church. As stated earlier, the majority of black families are headed by women.

In this fluid period, women will not find it easy to carve out independent careers and lifestyles *and* to maintain stable relationships with men. In one study of the characteristics of divorced and married women, the divorced women turned out to be significantly more aggressive and independent than the women who remained married.[7] Women, to a large extent, are victimized by the fact that the very same characteristics they need to obtain career mobility (assertiveness, strong achievement drive) are the ones which make it difficult to attract and hold a man. Thus, they are often placed in the position of a forced choice between career and marriage. And, men often place them in this position by their insistence on women playing supportive, not competitive, roles.

This practice may be defined as sexism. It is, also, a matter of personal choice that cannot be denied men. They have the right to choose women who meet their perceived needs, even if their exercise of that right limits the life options of women. In much the same way, women have the right to refuse to enter into a marriage or relationship of any kind that will not permit them freedom of expression. Some black men and women live in a union based on a quasi-equalitarian model. However, there can rarely be a completely equalitarian relationship between any two human beings. So, this is not really the issue. The issue is what, and who, determines the various kinds of inequalities that will exist in a male/female relationship?

One source of black male/female inequality lies in the shortage of black men, thus limiting the choices and alternatives of black women as well as exposing them to the abuse of black men keenly aware of that fact. However, before we decry the abuse of black women and the advantages black men achieve from this situation, it would behoove us to closely examine just how great an advantage it is. First, why is there a black male shortage since at birth the ratio of men to women is about equal? The answer lies in the higher morbidity and mortality rate of black men in the marriageable years. In the 15–30 age bracket black men have a mortality rate that is twice that of black women. Even sadder is the fact that homicide and suicide are two of the top three causes of death among them.[8] However, even the remaining black men suffer from serious problems. Almost a half million of them are behind bars; an estimated one-third of the black men in the inner city have a drug problem; and 25–50 percent of them are without steady employment.[9]

The black feminist thesis is that the last 50 years have seen a growing distrust, even hatred, between black men and women. They acknowledge that it is perpetuated by white racism but claim that black ignorance of the sexual politics of their experience in this country has played its part. However, it is a questionable conclusion that the addicted, imprisoned and unemployed black male is the main culprit in this scenario. In agreement with Pauline Stone, I acknowledge that "within Afro-American culture maleness creates privileges — that is, certain freedoms and rights are attached to being male."[10] However, she correctly attributes this to the societal strategy of manipulating blacks through the maintenance of sexual inequalities in the home and workplace. In both cases the main beneficiaries of the division that ensues are white male capitalists.

The divisive effect of sexism is a double edged sword. As psychiatrist Alvin Poussaint notes: "At the college level, particularly in black colleges, black females outnumber the males and (outdo them) in terms of achievement. That's going to tell you something about who's going to be achieving and moving into different spots. The white male and the white female feel much more threatened by the black male than by the black female, which may set up a condition for easier access."[11] There is every reason to believe that, by the turn of the 21st century, black women will exceed black men in terms of occupation and income. They already have more education. As for black men, their future is revealed in the statistic that of 23 million Americans who are functional illiterates, the highest proportions are among black males.[12]

Other feminists are critical of black women who choose to pursue an independent course but have children. Obviously, what is left is for the black woman to go it alone, without children or men as excess baggage, while she writes her own history. I just finished a study of middle class black singles, most of whom were women.[13] Many of them had become *de facto* practitioners of the feminist theory: they were alone, upwardly mobile, without man or child. The older they were, the less satisfactory was this condition. And, the reason why is simple enough. The male or female cannot stand alone and develop a sense of identity. It only makes sense, satisfies the soul, when it relates to some other role. To be ontological, humans are not meant to live out their lives alone with no higher purpose than self-satisfaction.

SEXISM AND BLACK FEMINISM

Sexism is an essential element in U.S. capitalist society and it is a force that corrupts and limits all the relationships that black men and women have with themselves and with each other. It is a very positive development that the criticism of sexism among black people has emerged. But it is only a beginning, and the dialectics have yet to be developed. Care must be taken not to blame the victims for actions which must be largely placed on the machinations of racism and capitalism. Black feminists must avoid actions which aid and abet these forces rather than contribute to the dialogue needed to iron out the differences between black men and women.

While many blacks are not opposed to feminism as a social movement nor black women as full, equal partners in all aspects of black life, we must be cognizant of the implications of feminism for an oppressed community. Female equality is more than a function of political and economic relationships. It involves personal relationships as well. Therefore, it reaches to the very core of human relationships, intruding into the most intimate aspects of our lives. Many of the inequalities that feminists perceive in male/female relationships cannot be corrected exclusively by governmental action, nor even by economic changes. They must be remedied through a combination of efforts, including the re-education of men and women and changes in sex-role socialization. It will not be resolved through acrimonious plays and books that place most of the blame for the conditions of black women at the feet of black men.

Because current black feminist analysis is often based on problems in interpersonal relationships, it, in many cases, is subjective. Personal relationships are never perfect, regardless of the political awareness of the persons involved. There are always difficulties, problems,and struggles. We must distinguish between such inevitable problems, and those that come directly from sexist abuse. Much of the popular feminist literature blurs the distinction between the inevitable difficulties that arise from human interaction, and those that stem directly from sexist motives. Moreover, some women give as much as they get. There are men, believe it or not, who have been abused or betrayed by women. Yet, they have no movement, no ideology, to articulate their role as oppressed beings; they are only the victims of their own culpability.

Much of contemporary black feminism is motivated by problems in interpersonal relationships, not political or economic domination by black males. That was the point in citing the statistics on single black women, interracial marriages and the imbalance in the sex ratio. While not all of black feminism stems from such factors, it is clear that much of it does. Even Michele Wallace admits to this in her statement that: "Some black women have come together because they can't find husbands. Some are angry with their boyfriends. The lesbians are looking for a public forum for their sexual preference. Others notice that if one follows in the footsteps of the white feminists, a lucrative position or promotion may come up before long."[14] While such motivations should not be used to discredit the legitimate grievances of black women, it does lend a complexity to the situation that does not confront other social problems.

What, in particular, diminishes the credibility of black feminism is the lack of balance between pure feminist ideology and the reality of the black community. The political and economic subordination of black women is a function of racism and capitalism, forces to which all blacks are subjected. It is primarily in the sphere of personal relations that changes in male behavior can occur and there is neither consensus nor consistency among black women about what those changes should be. Without a concise definition of black male sexism, each heterosexual dyad must work out its own definition of the resolution for sexual inequality. First, we must recognize that male sexism is a world view, not a conspiracy. It is a world view that places a woman's needs as always subordinate to the male's perquisites. This self-centered philosophy is a result of socialization processes that are many centuries old, often carried out by women, and internalized by virtually all people on this planet.

Women who have had their consciousness raised rightly expect the American creed of democracy to be extended to them. As long as male dominance was accepted as a God-given right, the exercise of male privilege created little subjective discomfort. Once women realize the constraints placed on their autonomy, their potential, it becomes more painful to those subjected to it. Yet, so much of white sexism has never had the same magnitude in the black community. Black women were in the labor market, received an education, participated in the decision making process and studies consistently show black men to have a less sexist attitude toward women's role than their white counterparts.[15] The remnants of sexist attitudes should be dealt with through education, communication and conciliation. Men should be sensitized to the need to participate equally in housework and child rearing, should cease the physical abuse of women, should accept the assertive black woman as an asset to his goals, and those of the community.

Meanwhile, we must be alert to the actual advancements black women are making and the effects of these advancements in an oppressed community. Witness, for example, the statistics which show that the ratio of white female to white male earnings decreased slightly between 1963 and 1974 (59 to 56 percent). During that same period of time, black women increased their income to the ratio of black male income, from 57 to 74 percent.[16] And, college educated black women have a higher median income than college educated white women.[17] In 1977 the black woman had 79 percent of the median annual income of black men. College educated black women, the majority of the black feminists, earn 90 percent of the annual median income of college educated black men.

There is nothing negative about this trend. In the main, black women are more educated, and often more competent. As long as their income is used in the service of the black community, and blacks remain united, there is little reason to fear their economic superiority over black males. The central point, moreover, is that given this trend it seems unnecessary to mount vicious public attacks on black men. We cannot avoid taking note of the fact that the black woman's ascendency in the labor force is, in part, white society's attempt to keep the black male in check. And, there is growing evidence that the black woman's progress, too, is being slowed by the tendency of white employers to favor white women for slots usually assigned to minorities.

POWER OR POVERTY:
THE BLACK MATRIARCHY REVISITED

One of the most familiar academic terms to black Americans is matriarchy. Originally, this concept was used to describe an entire society ruled by women. In the past thirty-five years it has been used to depict what many regard as a typical pattern of female dominance in the black family. This belief that black women rule the roost was strengthened by a study popularly known as the "Moynihan Report" which reached the conclusion that the "deterioration" of the black family was in large part due to the unnatural dominance of black women in a society where male control is the normal rule.[18]

Some years ago I wrote an article entitled "The Myth of the

Black Matriarchy" in which I asserted that this labeling of black women was a cruel hoax.[19] Two factors were given in Moynihan's document as examples of black matriarchy. One was the large number of female-headed households in the black community; the other was the disproportionate number of decisions black women made regarding important matters of family concern. My response to the former charge is that while there are a much larger number of female-headed households among blacks than whites, the majority of black families are headed by a male and a female adult. Moreover, there is little currency to the argument of female dominance if heading a household is the primary characteristic. After all, who does she have to dominate? And the problems of being the major breadwinner and a female overwhelmingly outweight the advantages.

In response to the assumption that because black women have greater participation in family decision-making they dominate black men, who have been reduced to irresponsible, and spineless caricatures, there is little evidence that this situation exists. In fact, as has been observed, black women are much more likely to feel powerless in their dealings with black males. Although they put up a visible and valiant fight against black male domination, they usually wind up losing many more battles than they win. Why, for example, would we speak of female dominance, when there are numerous situations where a black woman gives birth to a child out of wedlock and is saddled with the problems of raising the child while the father accepts no responsibility. It is also common knowledge among blacks that the male children often have greater value to the parents and are reared to expect certain advantages over women. And, the reality of the situation is that, as with white males, the system of male supremacy works to their benefit.

One of the reasons for black male dominance is simply the shortage of them. There are a number of factors responsible for the decrease in the supply of eligible black males. Among them are (1) the very large number of black men in prisons and the military, (2) a much higher rate of interracial dating and marriage among black men, (3) the high mortality rate of black men between the ages of 15–30, (4) more black men have become gay than black women, and (5) the increasing tendency of black males to remain unmarried.[20]

These factors also explain, in part, why there are so many more black female-headed households than in the white community. The Census Bureau reports that in 1978, 45 percent of all such families existed among blacks compared to only 13 percent for whites.[21] Because of the shortage of black males there is just no opportunity for all black women to form a monogamous family. Some estimates are that there is a shortfall of almost two million black males available for marriage. Added to the reasons already given, the higher rate of separation and divorce and out-of-wedlock births contribute to the large number of black female-headed households.

One should not assume any lack of desire to remain married or have legitimate children on the part of blacks from the above fact, rather their divorce rate is high because they are disproportionately concentrated in the low-income group where the marital break-up rate is highest. As for out-of-wedlock births, wide racial disparities in those rates continue to exist. Among the major reasons for this is the greater access of whites to contraceptive services. And, estimates that almost half of American marriages involve a pregnant bride indicate that we can make few valid statements about illegitimate births based on official records.[22]

It is this same group of black women who have been so adversely affected by the inflationary rise in consumer products and services. First, many of them receive their basic income from welfare and jobs which are not unionized. Thus, they have few ways of bringing their income in line with price increases. Secondly, blacks and particularly the poor, have been more seriously affected by the increased cost of certain items. A National Urban League study reveals that cost increases of such items as food, fuel and utilities had a greater impact on low-income black consumers since they pay a larger share of their income for them than do middle-income consumers.[23]

Another unfortunate result of the matriarchy myth is the negative image it projects onto black males, the majority of whom are living with and carrying out their family responsibilities. Even among the very low-income groups, the major breadwinner is most often the male. Perhaps it is time to put to rest these old and inaccurate stereotypes of black women and black men.

The real task before us remains an alleviation of the persistent forces of poverty and racial discrimination in employment opportunities. Until something effective is done to combat those problems, they, along with the aid of raging inflation, can only create more female-headed households. And, that means poverty — not power — for the women in them.

CLASS, CULTURE AND SEXISM

Much of the discussion of black feminism is a preoccupation of the middle class. Its concerns are not usually the concerns of poor and working class blacks. Lower class black women are burdened with low-income and the major responsibility for rearing children. And the men have been consigned to society's dumping grounds and have retreated to drug and alcohol abuse, suicide and unsuccessful careers of crime.

Arguing the relative weight of their oppression is a mere cavil. The issue of feminism reflects a crisis of the black bourgeoisie. James Baldwin, in commenting on Michele Wallace's book, noted; "I hazard that it (the sexual tension) is one of the symptoms of black middle-classdom. I doubt very much that the women I grew up with, my sister, my mother, I doubt very much that is their complaint . . . the inevitable tension, fury, always erupts against the one closest to you. But they understood that. That had nothing to do with our manhood as such. The anti-male thing which is now beginning seems to me to be one of the offshoots of the American dream as ingested by blacks."[24]

Certainly, it is a far cry from the black folk traditions of the South, where men and women, stormy relationships and all, worked and loved together, in the face of the constant, unrelenting pressures of racism. What appears to be happening, among the black bourgeoisie as they ascend the socio/economic scale, is the internalization of white values. Among these values will be sexism, materialism and individualism.

Thus, as the black male reaches middle class status he seeks the traditional passive, subordinate female model as a wife and avoids the self-actualizing assertive black woman. We have always had strong, independent black women in our midst. They are the mothers, the sisters, the daughters of the race. That is how blacks survived the travail of slavery and modern day racism. To reject them is the ultimate exercise in self-negation. The relaxation of the racial caste lines have led to our diversion from the larger struggle against racism and capitalism to secondary issues of sex role privileges, skin color and class divisions.

Some say the abolition of capitalism will not eliminate sexism. However, a rational economic system designed to meet social needs, not elicit profits for a small elite, will create the conditions where the need for sexist attitudes and practices will diminish. Otherwise, we will forever remain captives to the divide and conquer strategy of the ruling classes. While women should continue to fight sexism, it is folly to believe they can achieve full equality for over half of this country's population, with no changes in the political and economic order. Female separatism does not seem like a viable possibility and a struggle waged along gender lines in an oppressed community, contains the potential for defusing all larger struggles.

Either black women must accept the necessity of waging a tripartite struggle against sexism, racism and capitalism or continue to blame black men for all the problems they face. Although black men must accept some responsibility for their actions, much of what is happening is beyond their control. Black men are not such privileged creatures as many women seem to think, for there is a high price to be paid for being male in this society. Unwittingly, many black men do not realize the high price that they pay for their sexism. And, the highest price we may all pay, man and woman and child, is the destruction of our community. To avoid that fate, compassion and compromise are required on the part of all of us. We can neither achieve that objective by unfair and acrimonious charges of sexism against anyone who is male nor by persisting in unbridled male chauvinism. What we need is a universalistic ethos which will bind us as one, while simultaneously protecting our integrity as special and different entities. We stand at a point of crisis and this time it is the danger within which we must defeat.

SUMMARY

Ultimately the issue in America is not that of sexism or racism; it is monopoly capitalism and its impact on human potential. In terms of the Maoist concept of major and minor contradictions in a society, sexism and the problems black women face are derivatives of a larger contradiction between capital and labor. Sexism, as is racism, benefits the capitalist order by maintaining differentials in privileges and rewards within the working class. Some feminists, unfortunately, do not place the issue of black male sexism in any kind of theoretical framework, thus losing sight of the structural context in which sexism manifests itself. Indeed, the most glaring flaw in their ideology is the acceptance of the status quo in the degree to which capitalism is exonerated for the problems between black men and women. To completely ignore capitalism's systemic features, and its role in black oppression, is to adopt the normative approach of neoconservative social analysis and bias which is no different from that of whites.

If feminists placed their work in a perspective which was more global, rather than visceral and racially nationalistic, we might understand why black men exhibit these symptoms of sexism. Feminists speak, for example, of the growing distrust and hatred between black men and women in the last fifty years. Yet, they do not tell us why this distrust and hatred exists. Could it be that the urban industrial transition from the rural peasant culture sowed the seeds for the alienation of black men from their cultural moorings? In the South, black women were respected and men *helped* to provide for their families. As they came to the urban North, materialistic values gained ascendency. The symbols of manhood, sexual conquest, dominance of women, etc., became important to black men because they lacked the real symbols — political and economic power.

A most fatal flaw of the feminist thesis is the misreading of the life experience of blacks and a tendency to read into it the problems of the larger society. Because white women are opposed to the sexist behavior of white men in the form of their complete domination of them, some middle class black women assume the analogous counterpart can be found in black culture. But, the structural underpinnings for sexism are not the same in black society. The problem of some black feminists is, that being middle class, they were raised away from the realities of the black experience and tend to see it all as pathological in the same way that whites do. Many of these problems of interpersonal relations between black men and women are resolved in very creative and adaptive ways. The feminists put down working class black culture without really understanding it. The internal machinations of the capitalist order is sufficient reason to keep most black men and women together, if only in a symbiotic relationship.

The feminist polemic for all its flaws, has revealed some very truthful and painful issues, with which we have to deal. But, the politics of confrontation can be counter productive when practiced in a society of unequals. When all is said and done, it is not a matter of being male or female. It is, instead, a matter of people understanding that they are products of their culture and cannot free themselves from it for greater individual freedom unless they first understand the constraints that culture imposes. Thus, perspectives, one's own as they are derived from or freed from culture, largely determine what kinds of experiences men and women have with each other. Stated differently, we are a product of our cumulative experiences and the interpretations we give those experiences. Hence, experience, culture and perspective are essentially one, unless we consciously separate them, and most people do not. Feminists are correct when they say we must make our own history or remain victims of it. However, I think we should do it together.

Notes

FOOTNOTES FROM CHAPTER ONE

1. Michelle Wallace, *Black Macho and the Myth of the Superwoman*, (New York: Dial Press, 1979).
2. Denise Pauline, *Women of Tropical Africa*, (Berkeley: University of California Press, 1971).
3. Stanley Elkins, *Slavery: A Problem in American Institutional and Intellectual Life*, (Chicago: University of Chicago Press, 1959).
4. Alex Haley, *Roots*, (Garden City, New York: Doubleday, 1976).
5. John Blassingame, *The Slave Community*, (New York: Oxford University Press, 1972).
6. E. Franklin Frazier, *The Negro Family in the United States*, (Chicago: University of Chicago Press, 1939).
7. Eugene Genovese, "The Slave Family, Women — A Reassessment of Matriarchy," *Southern Voices* 1, (September, 1974), 16.
8. Herbert Gutman, *The Black Family in Slavery and Freedom 1750-1950*, (New York: Pantheon, 1976).
9. United States Bureau of the Census, "Divorce, Child Custody, and Child Support," Washington, D.C., United States Government Printing Office, 1979.
10. Carol Stack, *All Our Kin*, (New York: Harper and Row, 1974).
11. Robert Hill, *The Strengths of Black Families*, (New York: Emerson Hall, 1973).
12. John McCarthy and William Yancey, "Uncle Tom and Mr. Charlie: Metaphysical Pathos in the Study of Racism and Personal Disorganization," *American Journal of Sociology* 76 (January, 1971): 648-672.
13. Florence Halpern, *Survival: Black/White*, (New York: Pergamon, 1973).
14. Ronald Taylor, "Psychological Development of Black Youth," *Journal of Black Studies* 6 (June, 1976): 353-372.
15. Komelle Benjamin, *Factors Related to Conceptions of the Male Familial Role by Black Youth*, (State College, Mississippi: Mississippi State University Press, 1971).
16. Douglas Glasgow, *The Black Underclass*, (San Francisco: Jossey Bass, 1980).
17. United States Bureau of the Census, "Estimates of the Population of the United States by Age, Race and Sex: 1976 to 1979," Washington, D.C.: United States Government Printing Office, 1980.
18. United States Bureau of the Census, "Educational Attainment in the United States: March 1979 and 1978," Washington, D.C.: United States Government Printing Office, 1980.
19. "Some Bad News on Jobless Rates of U.S. Youth," *The San Francisco Chronicle*, August 3, 1980, page 2.
20. "Black Unemployment Higher, Survey Shows," *The San Francisco Sunday Examiner*, August 3, 1980, page 2.
21. United States Bureau of the Census, "The Social and Economic Status of the Black Population in the United States: An Historical View 1790-1978," Washington, D.C.: United States Government Printing Office, 1979.
22. Bernard Weinaub, "Military Wages War on Racism's Persistent Shadow," *The New York Times*, October, 1979, page 4E.
23. Winthrop Jordan, *White Over Black: American Attitudes Toward the Negro 1550-1812*, (Durham, N.C.: University of North Carolina Press, 1968).

24. Clemont Vontress, "The Black Male Personality," *The Black Scholar* (June, 1971): 10–17.
25. William Grier and Price Cobbs, *Black Rage,* (New York: Basic Books, 1968).
26. Carlfred Broderick, "Social Heterosexual Development Among Urban Negroes and Whites," *Journal of Marriage and the Family,* 27 (May, 1965): 200–203; David Larson, et. al., "Social Factors in the Frequency of Romantic Involvement Among Adolescents," *Adolescence* II (Spring, 1976): 7–12; Leanor B. Johnson, "Sexual Behavior of Southern Blacks," in *The Black Family, Essays and Studies,* Robert Staples, Ed. (Belmont, California: Wadsworth, 1978):80–92.
27. L. Johnson, Ibid.
28. Kenneth Clark, *Dark Ghetto,* (New York: Harper and Row, 1965).
29. Charles Stember, *Sexual Racism,* (New York: Elsevier Press, 1976).
30. Gary Schulman, "Race, Sex and Violence: A Laboratory Test of the Sexual Threat of the Black Male Hypothesis," *American Journal of Sociology* 79 (March, 1974):1260–1277.
31. Paul Glick and Karen Mills, *Black Families: Marriage Patterns and Living Arrangements,* (Atlanta: Atlanta University Press, 1974).
32. United States Bureau of the Census, "Marital Status and Living Arrangements: March, 1979," Washington, D.C.: United States Government Printing Office, 1980.
33. John Scanzoni, "Sex Roles, Economic Factors, and Marital Solidarity," *Journal of Marriage and the Family,* 37 (February, 1975): 130–144.
34. Ruth McKay, "One Child Families and Atypical Sex Ratios in an Elite Black Community," in *The Black Family: Essays and Studies,* Robert Staples ed. (Belmont, Calif.: Wadsworth, 1978), 177–181.
35. Elliot Liebow, *Tally's Corner,* (Boston: Little, Brown & Company, 1967).
36. Stack, op. cit.
37. John Scanzoni, *The Black Family in Modern Society,* (Boston: Allyn and Bacon, 1971).
38. Taylor, op. cit.
39. Noel Cazanave, "Middle-Income Black Fathers: An Analysis of the Provider Role," *The Family Coordinator* 28 (October, 1979): 583–593; Jealean Daneal, "A Definition of Fatherhood as Expressed by Black Fathers," unpublished Ph.D. dissertation, University of Pittsburgh, 1975.
40. United States Bureau of the Census, "The Social and Economic Status of the Black Population," op. cit.
41. National Black Feminist Organization Statement, 1973.
42. "Black Men Leaving Media," Brown, *The Los Angeles Sentinel,* December 11, 1980, page A-13.

FOOTNOTES FROM CHAPTER TWO

1. Herbert Gutman, *The Black Family in Slavery and Freedom 1750–1925*, (New York: Pantheon, 1976).
2. Douglas Glasgow, *The Black Underclass*, (San Francisco: Jossey-Bass, 1979).
3. United States Bureau of the Census, "Estimates of the Population of the United States, by Age, Race, and Sex: 1976 to 1979," Washington, D.C.: United States Government Printing Office, 1980.
4. Alfred Malabre, Jr., "Recession Hits Blacks Harder than Whites, Widening the Pay Gap," *The Wall Street Journal*, August 21, 1980, page 1.
5. *Los Angeles Sentinel*, April 10, 1975, page A-2, quoted from, "Black Teens Unemployed."
6. Malabre, loc. cit.
7. Leanor B. Johnson and Robert Staples, "Family Planning and the Young Minority Male: A Pilot Project," *The Family Coordinator* 28, (October 1979): 535–543.
8. Bernard Weinraub, "Military Wages War on Racism's Persistent Shadow," *The New York Times*, October 7, 1979, page 4E. An unemployment rate of 18 percent in 1980 among black college graduates undoubtedly accounted for the increase (it was 2.8 percent in 1975) of blacks in the officer ranks.
9. Norma Chapman and George Jordan, "Non-Honorable Discharges and Blacks: Military Justice," *The Urban League Review*, (Spring 1975) 22–25.
10. Michael Getler, "Blacks and The U.S. Army," *San Francisco Sunday Examiner and Chronicle*, This World Section, September 2, 1973, page 16.
11. National Urban League Research Department, "Quarterly Economic Report on the Black Worker," May 1975, page 2.
12. There were cases where whites were admitted into the army with lower scores than black candidates. As the joblessness rate of whites declined, so did their numbers in the Volunteer Army. The large number of blacks in the U.S. Army prompted the statement by former Israeli Defense Minister Moshe Dayan that "The U.S. Armed Forces are made up of blacks who have low intelligence." Quoted from *The San Francisco Chronicle*, November 27, 1980, page 7.
13. Grace Massey, et. al., "Racism Without Racists: Institutional Racism in Urban Schools," *The Black Scholar* (November 1975) pages 10–19.
14. "23 Million Incompetent Americans," *The San Francisco Chronicle* October 29, 1975, page 1.
15. "HEW Backs Down," *Newsweek*, October 27, 1975, page 66.
16. Alfred S. Arkley, "Integration and Political Growth," paper presented at the American Political Science Association Meeting, New York, 1973.
17. "School Violence-Vandalism," *The Black Child Advocate* 4, (May 1975) page 5.
18. Audrey L. Johnson, "The Legitimation of Violence: Political Socialization and the New Gangs," a paper presented to the InterAmerican Congress of Criminology, Caracus, Venezeula, November, 1972.
19. Frantz Fanon, *A Dying Colonialism*, (New York: Grove Press, 1967) pages 121–124.
20. Frantz Fanon, *The Wretched of the Earth*, (New York: Grove Press, 1963).
21. "Number of Blacks Attending College Triples in Decade," *The Washington Post*, June 10, 1978, page A-1.

22. Reynolds Farley, "Death by Murder: An Analysis of Racial Similarities and Differences in Homocide," paper presented at the American Sociological Association Meeting, August 1978, San Francisco.
23. United States Department of Health, Education and Welfare, National Center for Health Statistics, Monthly Vital Statistics Report, "Final Mortality Statistics 1977," March 30, 1978, page 26.
24. Farley, op. cit.
25. United States Bureau of the Census, "The Social and Economic Status of the Black Population in the United States, 1974," Washington, D.C.: United States Government Printing Office, 1975, page 165. The proportion of black males in jail was even higher in 1980, and they only represent 5 percent of the total population in the United States.
26. Douglass Cater and Stephen Stricklan, TV Violence and the Child, (New York: Russell Sage, 1975).
27. Alphonso Pinkney, The American Way of Violence, (New York: Random House, 1972).
28. Frantz Fanon, The Wretched of the Earth, op. cit. page 31.
29. Nathan Goldman, "The Differential Selection of Juvenile Offenders for Court Appearances" in Crime and the Legal Process, W. Chambers, Ed., (New York: McGraw-Hill, 1969) pages 264–294.
30. "1 of 10 Addicted in Parts of the Inner City," The Washington Post, April 4, 1972, page C-1.
31. William Earl Berry, "How Drugs are Used to Rip Off the Black Community," Jet, August 10, 1972, pages 22–29.
32. One study estimates that 130,000 heroin addicts are black high school graduates, a disproportionate 60 percent of all addicts with high school displomas. c.f. Williams A. Darity, "Alcohol and other Drugs as Cripplers," a paper presented at the annual meeting of the National Urban League, July 1977, Washington, D.C.
33. United States Department of Health, Education and Welfare, "Final Mortality Statistics," op. cit.
34. "Vital Statistics of the United States, 1970–1975," Washington, D.C.: United States Government Printing Office, 1975, tables 1–26.
35. Ibid.
36. Ibid.
37. Richard Seiden, "We're Driving Young Blacks to Suicide," Psychology Today, 4 (August 1970) pp. 24–28.
38. "Vital Statistics of the United States 1970–1975," op. cit.
39. Seiden, loc. cit.
40. Emile Durkheim, Suicide, (Glencoe, Illinois: The Free Press, 1952).
41. Warren Breed, "The Negro and Fatalistic Suicide," Pacific Sociological Review 13 (Summer 1970):156–162.
42. James Baldwin, The Fire Next Time, (New York: Dial Press, 1963).

FOOTNOTES FROM CHAPTER THREE

1. Gina Lombroso, Ferrero, *Criminal Man According to the Classifications of Cesare Lombroso*, (New York: Putnam, 1911).
2. C.F. Marvin Wolfgang and Bernard Cohen, *Crime and Race: Conceptions and Misconceptions*, (New York: Institute of Human Relations Press, 1970).
3. Frantz Fanon, *The Wretched of the Earth*, (New York: Grove Press, 1966); Robert Blauner, *Racial Oppression in America*, (New York: Harper and Row, 1972); Stokely Carmichael and Charles Hamilton, *Black Power*, (New York: Vintage Books, 1967); Albert Memmi, *The Colonizer and the Colonized*, (Boston: Beacon Press, 1967).
4. Freda Adler, *Sisters in Crime* (New York: McGraw Hill, 1975). Within the small number of female prisoners, black women represent a larger proportion of women imprisoned than do their black male counterparts.
5. Julius Lester, *Look Out, Whitey: Black Power's Gon' Get Your Mama*, (New York: Dial Press) 1968, p. 23.
6. C.f. Mary Berry, *Black Resistance–White Law: A History of Constitutional Racism in America* (New York: Appleton-Century Crofts, 1971).
7. "White Collar Crime is Everyone's Problem, Everyone's Loss," Washington, D.C. Chamber of Commerce of the United States of America, 1974.
8. Report of the Consumer Product Safety Commission, quoted in *Newsweek*, October 15, 1973, p. 91.
9. Stephen Bennett and Alfred Tuchfarber, "The Social Structural Sources of Cleavage on Law and Order Policies, America,'" *Journal of Political Science*, 19 (August 1975):419–438.
10. Fanon, op. cit., p. 31.
11. Wallace Mendelson, *Discrimination*, (Englewood Cliffs, New Jersey: Prentice-Hall, 1962) pp. 143–144.
12. Albert J. Reiss, Jr., "Police Brutality-Answers to Key Questions," *Transaction* (July–August 1968), 10–19.
13. Testimony of Dr. Evrum Mendelsohn of the Elmhurst Psychological Center before Congressman Ralph Metcalfe's Public Hearings on Police Brutality in Chicago, September 1, 1972.
14. Gunnar Myrdal, *An American Dilemma*, (New York: Harper and Brothers, 1944) p. 542.
15. Patrick Osten, "Find Black Men Most Likely to be Shot by Cops," *Chicago Sun-Times*, May 16, 1977, p. 4.
16. *Report of the National Advisory Commission on Civil Disorders*, op. cit., p. 302.
17. Ibid., p. 268.
18. "D.C. Black Cops Don't Trust Fellow White Cops, *Jet Magazine*, March 11, 1976, p. 5.
19. "N.Y.'s Black Cops Quit Police Union," *The San Francisco Chronicle*, December 9, 1976, p. 38.
20. Lynn Ludlow, "Hongisto, Garner: Rampant Racism in SFPD," *The San Francisco Examiner*, October 30, 1977, p. 1.
21. Louis Lomax, *The Negro Revolt*, (New York: New American Library, 1962) p. 59.
22. F.B.I. Uniform Crime Report, "Crime in the United States: 1978" Federal Bureau of Investigation, Washington, D.C. 1979, p. 207.

23. Law Enforcement Assistance Administration, "Criminal Victimization in the United States: January-June 1973" Washington, D.C.: U.S. Government Printing Office, November, 1974, Vol. 1, p. 3.
24. Fanon, op. cit., p. 43.
25. "Study Shows Executions Used Mostly for Killers of Whites," Poverty Law Report, Spring 1978, p. 2.
26. Henry A. Bullock, "Significance of the Racial Factor in the Length of Prison Sentences," The Journal of Criminal Law, Criminology and Police Science 7, (November 1961):411-417.
27. "Law Suppresses Minorities, Panel Says," The San Francisco Chronicle, October 18, 1980, p. 6.
28. Cited in "Civil Rights Update," United States Commission on Civil Rights, November, 1978, p. 2.
29. Richard P. McGlynn, James C. Megas and Daniel Benson, "Sex and Race as Factors Affecting the Attribution of Insanity in a Murder Trial," Journal of Psychology 93 (April 1976):93-99.
30. Fanon, "Culture and Racism" in Toward the African Revolution, New York: Monthly Review Press, 1967, p. 40.
31. Marilyn Elias, "Bias In The Jury Box," The San Francisco Sunday Examiner and Chronicle, This World Section, June 29, 1980, p. 32.
32. Daniel Swett, "Cross-Cultural Communications in the Courtroom. Applied Linguistics in a Murder Trial," a paper presented at the Conference on Racism and the Law, San Francisco, December, 1967.
33. Stuart Nagel, The Legal Process From a Behavioral Perspective (Homewood, Illinois: Dorsey, 1969).,
34. Cited in Hugo Bedau, The Death Penalty in America, (New York 1967), p. 411.
35. Marilyn Elias, "Blind Justice and Color," The San Francisco Sunday Examiner and Chronicle, This World Section, December 30, 1977, pp. 24-25.
36. "Study Shows Executions Used Mostly for Killers of Whites," loc. cit.
37. "A Profile of Who's on Death Row," The San Francisco Chronicle, November 29, 1976, p. 12.
38. Garry Mendez, "Crime: A Major Problem in Black America" in The State of Black America 1980, New York: National Urban League, 1980, p. 224.
39. Angela Davis, "The Soledad Brothers," The Black Scholar, (April-May 1971) pp. 2-3.
40. Mendez, op. cit., p. 225.
41. "Prisoners Ordered to End Racial Use of Discipline," Poverty Law Report, January/February, 1979, p. 3.
42. Jessica Mitford, Kind and Usual Punishment: The Prison Business (New York: Knopf, 1973).
43. "Guinea Pig Experiments Are Conducted in Prisons," Jet Magazine, August 24, 1972, p. 20.
44. Robert Chrisman, "Black Prisoners, White Law," The Black Scholar, (April-May 1971) pp. 45-46.
45. Issac Balbul, The Dialectics of Legal Repression, (New York: Russell Sage, 1973) p. 5.

FOOTNOTES FROM CHAPTER FOUR

1. H. Rap Brown, *Die, Nigger, Die,* (New York: Dial Press, 1969).
2. Hugh Graham and Ted Gurr, (eds.) *Violence in America,* (New York: Signet, 1969).
3. Frantz Fanon, Preface *The Wretched of the Earth,* (New York: Grove Press, 1963) p. 22.
4. Alphonso Pinkney, *The American Way of Violence,* (New York: Random House, 1972) p. 26.
5. Joe B. Frantz, "The Frontier Tradition: An Invitation to Violence" in *Violence in America,* op.cit., pp. 119–143.
6. Pinkney, op. cit.
7. C. Wright Mills, *The Power Elite,* (New York: Oxford University Press, 1956) p. 184.
9. Report of the Consumer Product Safety Commission quoted in *Newsweek,* October 15, 1973, p. 91. This is three times the number of homicide victims in a year.
10. Marvin Wolfgang and Bernard Cohen, *Crime and Race,* (New York: Institute of Human Relations Press, 1970) p. 44.
11. Basil Davidson, *The African Slave Trade,* (Boston: Little, Brown and Co., 1959).
12. Stanley Elkins, *Slavery,* (New York: Grosset and Dunlap, 1959).
13. Frederic Wertham, *A Sign for Cain: An Exploration of Human Violence,* (New York: Macmillan, 1966) p. 91.
14. Bureau of the Census, *Historical Statistics of the United States, Colonial Times to 1957.* Washington, D.C., U.S. Government Printing Office, 1960, p. 218.
15. Gunnar Myrdal, *An American Dilemma,* (New York: Harper and Brothers, 1944) p. 567.
16. The pendulum has turned again. At the beginning of the eighties, there were a rash of white attacks on blacks in some American cities.
17. Gina Lombroso, Ferrers, *Criminal Man According to the Classifications of Cesare Lombroso,* (New York: Putnam, 1911).
18. Ashley Montague, *Man's Most Dangerous Myth: The Fallacy of Race,* (New York: World, 1964).
19. Marvin Wolfgang and F. Ferracuti, *The Subculture of Violence,* (London: Social Science Paperbacks, 1967).
20. Thomas Pettigrew and Rosalind Spier, "The Ecological Structure of Negro Homicide," *American Journal of Sociology,* 67, (May, 1962). pp. 621–629.
21. Elkins, op. cit.
22. P. Everts and K. Schwirian, "Metropolitan Crime Rates and Relative Deprivation," *Criminologica* 5 (1968) pp. 43–52.
23. Walter Miller, "Lower Class Culture as a Generating Millieu of Gang Delinquency," *Journal of Social Issues.* 14 (Fall, 1958) pp. 5–19.
24. Leonard Savitz, "Black Crime" in *Comparative Studies of Blacks and Whites in the United States,* Kent Miller and Ralph Dreger, eds., (New York: Seminar Press, 1973) pp. 467–516.
25. Robert Staples, "The Myth of the Black Matriarchy," *The Black Scholar,* (January, 1970) pp. 8–16.

26. Marvin E. Wolfgang, *Patterns in Criminal Homicide*, (New York: John Wiley and Sons, 1958) pp. 200–207. More recent studies have come up with similar figures.

27. Federal Bureau of Investigation, "Crime in the United States, 1972," Crime Reports, Washington, D.C., U.S. Government Printing Office, 1973, Table 36, p. 131.

28. Ibid.

29. Paul Bohannon, ed. *African Homicide and Suicide*, (New York: Atheneum, 1967) p. 237.

30. Frantz Fanon, *The Wretched of the Earth*, (New York: Grove Press, 1963) pp. 29–74.

31. Grahm B. Spanier and Carol Fishel, "The Housing Project and Familial Functions: Consequences for Low Income Families," *The Family Coordinator*, 23 (April 1973) pp. 235–240.

32. Claude Brown, *Manchild in the Promised Land*, (New York: Macmillan, 1965) pp. 263–271.

33. Alphonso Pinkney, *The American Way of Violence*, (New York: Random House, 1972) pp. 3–37.

34. William J. Bowers, *Executions in America*, (Lexington, Mass: Lexington Books, 1974) p. 78.

35. Winthrop Jordan, *White Over Black: American Attitudes Toward the Negro 1550-1812*, (Durham, North Carolina, University of North Carolina Press, 1968).

36. John M. Macdonald, *Rape Offenders and Their Victims* (Springfield, Illinois. Charles C. Thomas, 1971).

37. Michael W. Agapian, et. al., "Interracial Rape in a North American City: An Analysis of 66 Cases," a paper presented to the Inter-American Congress of Criminologists, Caracus, Venezuela, November 1972, p. 13.

38. Myrdal, op. cit., p. 65.

39. Fanon, *Wretched of the Earth*, op. cit., p. 32.

40. Eldrige Cleaver, *Soul on Ice*, (New York: McGraw-Hill, 1968) p. 26.

41. Ralph Ginzburg, *100 Years of Lynching* (New York: Lancer Books, 1962).

42. William J. Bowers, loc. cit.

43. Savitz, op. cit., p. 482.

44. Boone Hammond, "The Contest System: A Survival Technique," Masters thesis, Washington University, 1965, p. 38.

45. Joyce Ladner, *Tomorrow's Tomorrow: The Black Woman*, (Garden City, New York: Doubleday, 1971) pp. 51–52.

46. Bernette Golden, cited in "The Ugly Crime of Rape," *Essence*, 6 (June 1974), p. 37.

47. Carolyn Jetter Greene, *70 Soul Secrets of Sapphire*, (San Francisco: Sapphire Publishing Co., 1973) p. 6.

48. Menachim Amir, "Sociocultural Factors in Forcible Rape," in *Sexual Behavior* (Leonard Gross, ed.) New York: Spectrum Publications, 1974, p. 12.

49. Germaine Greer, "Seduction is a Four Letter Word," *Playboy*, January, 1973, pp. 220–223.

50. Dotson Rader, "The Sexual Nature of Violence," *The New York Times*, October 22, 1973, p. 231.

51. Murray Straus et. al., *Behind Closed Doors: Violence in the American Family* (Garden City, New York: Anchor, 1980).
52. Noel Cazanave and Murray Straus, "Race, Class, Network Embeddedness and Family Violence: A Search for Potent Support Systems," *Journal of Comparative Family Studies* 10 (Fall 1979): 281-300.
53. St. Clair Drake and Horace Cayton, *Black Metropolis,* (New York: Harcourt, Brace and Co., 1945) pp. 566-67.
54. Cazanave and Straus, op. cit.
55. B.D. Cohen, "Home Fights Hurt Hundreds," *The Washington Post,* March 25, 1973, p. 81 — 3.
56. C.f. Robert Staples, *The Black Woman in America: Sex, Marriage and the Family,* (Chicago: Nelson-Hall, 1973) pp. 114.
57. David A. Schutz, *Coming Up Black: Patterns of Ghetto Socialization,* (Englewood Cliffs, New Jersey: Prentice-Hall, 1969) p. 107.
58. Bohannon, op. cit. p. 244.
59. Greene, op. cit. p. 45.
60. James Boudouris, "Homicide and The Family," *Journal of Marriage and the Family,* Vol. 33 (November 1971), p. 671.
61. Cazqanave and Straus, loc. cit.
62. Wolfgang, loc. cit.
63. William Goode, "Force and Violence in the Family," *Journal of Marriage and the Family,* 33 (November 1971), p. 33.
64. Reuben Hill and Howard Becker, eds., *Family, Marriage and Parenthood,* (Boston, D.C. Heath, 1975) p. 790.
65. Lee Rainwater, *Behind Ghetto Walls,* (Chicago: Aldine, 1970) p. 163.
66. James D. Comer, "The Dynamics of Black and White Violence" in *Violence in America,* High Graham and Ted Gurr, ed., (New York: 1969), p. 434.
67. Alvin Poussaint, *Why Blacks Kill Blacks,* (New York: Emerson-Hall, 1972) p. 72.
68. Staples, *The Black Woman in America,* op. cit., Chapter 6.
69. Davis Gil, "Violence Against Children," *Journal of Marriage and the Family,* 33 (November 1971) p. 640.
70. Ibid.
71. Constance K. Kamis and Norma J. Radin, "Class Differences in the Socialization Practices of Negro Mothers" in *The Black Family: Essays and Studies,* Robert Staples, ed., (Belmont, California: Wadsworth, 1971), pp. 230-247.
72. Gil, op. cit., p. 648.
73. Cazanave and Straus, loc. cit.
74. Allison Davis and John Dollard, *Children of Bondage,* (Washington, D.C.: American Council on Education, 1940) pp. 264-267.
75. Cazanave and Straus, loc. cit.
76. "Crime in the United States," 1972, op. cit., p. 132.
77. Robert Staples, "To Be Young, Black and Oppressed," *The Black Scholar,* (December 1975) pp. 2-9.

174 | BLACK MASCULINITY

FOOTNOTES FROM CHAPTER FIVE

1. Robert Staples, "The Mystique of Black Sexuality," *Liberator* 7 (March 1967) p. 10.
2. Morton Hunt, *Sexual Behavior in the 1970's* (Chicago: Playboy Press, 1974).
3. Frantz Fanon, *Black Skin, White Masks,* (New York: Grove Press, 1967) p. 177.
4. Winthrop D. Jordan, *Black Over White: American Attitudes Toward The Negro, 1550–1812,* (Chapel Hill: University of North Carolina Press, 1968) pp. 34–35.
5. G. Rattray Taylor, *Sex in History* (New York: Ballantine Books, 1954).
6. Frederich Engels, *The Origin of the Family, Private Property and the State* (Chicago: Charles H. Kerr, 1902).
7. Boris De Rachewiltz, *Black Eros: Sexual Customs of Africa from Prehistory to the Present Day* (New York: Lyle Stuart, 1964).
8. Eugene Genovese, *Roll, Jordan, Roll,* (New York: Random House, 1975) pp. 458–475.
9. Jessie Barnard, *Marriage and Family Among Negroes,* (Englewood Cliffs: New Jersey: Prentice-Hall, 1966) p. 75.
10. Calvin Hernton, *Sex and Racism in America,* (Garden City, New York: Doubleday, 1965) p. 111–112.
11. Sigmund Freud, *The Basic Writings of Sigmund Freud,* Trans. by A.A. Brill (New York: Modern Library, 1938).
12. Reiche Reimut, *Sexuality and the Class Struggle* (Germany: NLB, 1970).
13. Robert Staples, *The Black Woman in America. Sex, Marriage and the Family* (Chicago: Nelson-Hall, 1973).
14. Calvin Hernton, *Coming Together,* (New York: Random House, 1971) pp. 17–19.
15. E. Franklin Frazier, "Sex Life of the African and American Negro" in *The Encyclopedia of Sexual Behavior* (A. Ellis and A. Abaranel eds.) New York: Hawthorn Books, 1961, pp. 769–775.
16. Raymond Walters, *The New Negro on Campus,* (Princeton, New Jersey: Princeton University Press, 1975) p. 37.
17. John F. Kantner and Melvin Zelnik, "Contraception and Pregnancy: Experience of Young Unmarried Women in the United States." *Family Planning Perspectives.* 4(October, 1972) p. 9–17.
18. Alan P. Bell, "Black Sexuality, Fact and Fancy" in *The Black Family: Essays and Studies,* Vol. 11, R. Staples, ed. (Belmont: Wadsworth 1978), pp. 77–79.
19. Boone F. Hammond, *The Contest System: A Survival Technique,* Masters essay. Washington University, 1965.
20. Robert Staples, "Race and Family Violence: The Internal Colonialism Perspective" in *Crime and its Impact on the Black Community,* L. Gary and L. Brown, ed. Washington, D.C. The Institute for Urban Affairs and Research, 1976, pp. 85–96.
21. Leanor B. Johnson, "Sexual Behavior of Southern Blacks" in *The Black Family: Essays and Studies,* Vol. II., op. cit. pp. 80–92.

Notes | 175

22. Current Population Reports, *Population Estimates and Projections.* Series p. 25, no. 643. U.S. Government Printing Office, 1977: The real sex ratio is actually closer to 85:100. My effective sex ratio only includes men available and compatible to most black women.
23. Anthony Pietropinto and Jacqueline Simenauer, *Beyond The Male Myth,* Quadrangle, 1977.
24. Johnson, op. cit.
25. Hunt, op. cit., p. 198.
26. U.S. Bureau of the Census, "Marital Status and Living Arrangements, Series," p. 20, No. 306, U.S. Government Printing Office, Washington, D.C. 1981.
27. Ibid. Between 1970-79, the divorce rate among blacks increased by 130 percent.
28. Joseph Scott, "Black Polygamous Family Formation: Caste Studies of Legal Wives and Consensual Wives," *Alternative Lifestyles* 3 (May 1980): 41-64.

FOOTNOTES FROM CHAPTER SIX

1. Works of Aristotle, *Friendship,* Encyclopedia Britannica, Volume 2, 1959, p. 459.
2. Louis M. Verborugge, "Multiplexity in Adult Friendships," paper presented at the American Sociological Association Meeting, New York, August 1976.
3. John S. Mbiti, *Love and Marriage in Africa,* (London: Longman, 1973) p. 35.
4. Robert Staples, "The Myth of the Impotent Black Male," *The Black Scholar* (June 1971): 2-9.
5. Thomas Pettigrew, *A Profile of the Negro American,* (Princeton, New Jersey: D. Van Nostrand, 1964) pp. 17-22.
6. E. Franklin Frazier, *Black Bourgeoisie,* (New York, Crowell-Collier, 1962) p. 182.
7. Pettigrew, loc. cit.
8. Personal communication from Wardell Pomeroy, former Associate Director of the Institute for Sex Research, November, 1971.
9. Quoted in the *San Francisco Chronicle,* October 27, 1976, p. 16.
10. Quoted in the *San Francisco Chronicle,* May 19, 1979, p. 33.
11. Alan Bell and Martin Weinberg, *Homosexualities,* (New York: Simon and Schuster, 1978) pp. 34-215.
12. Ibid, p. 173.
13. Ibid, p. 85.
14. Levi Benton, "Case History: I'm a Black Homosexual," *Sexology,* March 1972, pp. 15-18.
15. "Minorities Charging Gay Bars with Bias," The *San Francisco Chronicle,* November 23, 1980, p. 9.
16. "Religious Leaders Say Black Church Untouched by Gay Rights Crusade," *Jet Magazine,* June 13, 1978, p. 8.
17. Jocelyn Johnson, "Faggots, Freaks and Macho Men," *The Hilltop.* February 9, 1979, p. 5.
18. Bell and Weinberg, op. cit. pp. 63-4.
19. Ibid, p. 85.
20. Ibid, p. 117.
21. Ibid, p. 104.
22. Ibid, p. 207.
23. Audre Lorde, "Scratching the Surface: Some Notes on Barriers to Women and Loving," *The Black Scholar,* (April 1978) p. 34.
24. Ann Allen Schockley and Veronica Tucker, "Black Women Discuss Today's Problems: Men, Families, Society," *Southern Voices,* 1 (August–September 1974) p. 18.
25. Bell and Weinberg, op. cit., p. 93.
26. Ibid, p. 105.
27. Sex Team Finds Few Surprises in New Study, *The San Francisco Examiner,* April 17, 1979, p. 6.
28. Bell and Weinberg, ibid, pp. 183-184.
29. Ibid, p. 215.
30. Bid, p. 167.
31. Quoted in *The Sun Reporter,* August 30, 1979, p. 16.
32. Quoted in the *San Francisco Sunday Examiner and Chronicle* January 20, 1980, p. c-7.

FOOTNOTES FROM CHAPTER SEVEN

1. U.S. Bureau of the Census, "Marital Status and Living Arrangements: March 1980," Washington, D.C.: U.S. Government Printing Office, 1981.
2. Suzanne Bianchi and Reynolds Farley, "Racial Differences in Family Living Arrangements and Economic Well Being: An Analysis of Recent Trends," *Journal of Marriage and the Family* 41 (August 1979): 537–552.
3. Herbert Gutman, *The Black Family in Slavery and Freedom 1750–1925* (New York: Pantheon, 1976).
4. U.S. Bureau of the Census, "Marital Status and Living Arrangements: March 1973," Washington, D.C., U.S. Government Printing Office, 1974.
5. Paul C. Glick and Karen Mills, *Black Families: Marriage Patterns and Living Arrangements* (Atlanta: Atlanta University, 1974) p. 9.
6. U.S. Bureau of the Census, "Current Population Reports, Series p. 20, No. 314, Washington, D.C.: U.S. Government Printing Office, 1978, p. 31. Most of the men in that class, however, are married.
7. Ibid.
8. Graham Spanier and Paul Glick, "Mate Selection Differentials Between Whites and Blacks in the United States," *Social Forces* 58 (August 1980).
9. U.S. Bureau of the Census, "Marital Status and Living Arrangements: March 1980, op. cit.
10. Ibid.
11. Quoted in Dan Dorfman, "Tempest in the Take-Out Game," *San Francisco Examiner*, November 18, 1979, p. 3–13.
12. Ibid. Some very exclusive restaurants hand the female member of the duo a menu without prices listed, a practice that has drawn the protests of some feminists.
13. C.f. Beth Trier, "Beauty — Is It Only Pocketbook Deep?" *San Francisco Chronicle*, June 12, 1980, p. 43.
14. Bianchi and Farley, op. cit.
15. "Home Buying Needs Working Wife," *The San Francisco Sunday Examiner and Chronicle*, May 18, 1980, p. 34.
16. "S.F. Economist Traces Housing Crisis," *The San Francisco Sunday Examiner and Chronicle*, April 20, 1980.
17. Frederick Engels, *The Origin of the Family, Private Property, and the State* (Chicago: Charles W. Kerr, 1920).
18. Lee Rainwater, *Behind Ghetto Walls*, (Chicago: Aldine, 1970) p. 63.
19. Ibid.
20. Robert Bell, "Comparative Attitudes About Marital Sex Among Negro Women in the United States, Great Britain, and Trinidad," *Journal of Comparative Family Studies I.* (Autumn); 71–81.
21. Rainwater, *Behind Ghetto Walls*, (Chicago, Aldine, 1970) p. 63.
22. William M. Chavis and Gladys J. Lyles, "Divorce Among Educated Black Women," *Journal of the National Medical Association* 67, (March 1975): 128–134.
23. Bernard Farber, *Kinship and Family Organization* (New York: John Wiley and

Sons, 1966).

24. "Sex Lives of Cosmopolitan Readers," *The San Francisco Chronicle*, August 4, 1980, p. 1.
25. Ibid.
26. Lewis Yablonsky, "How Infidelity Can Strengthen Ailing Marriages," *The Detroit Free Press*, February 15, 1979, p. 5-C.
27. Robert Staples, *The World of Black Singles: Changing Patterns of Male-Female Relations* (Westport, Connecticut: Greenwood Press, 1981).
28. Patrice Rushen quoted in *Jet Magazine*, April 10, 1980, p. 30.

FOOTNOTES FROM CHAPTER EIGHT

1. Calvin Hernton, *Sex and Racism in America* (Garden City, New York: Doubleday, 1965).
2. Gunnar Myrdal, *An American Dilemma,* (New York: Harper and Row, 1944) pp. 60–61.
3. E. Franklin Frazier, *The Negro Family in the United States,* (Chicago: University of Chicago Press, 1939) pp. 50–51.
4. Frantz Fanon, *Black Skin, White Masks,* (New York: Grove Press, 1967) p. 163.
5. Susan Berman, "San Francisco, City of Sin: Why Can't I Get Laid?" *City of San Francisco,* (August 3, 1975) p. 10.
6. Doris Y. Wilkinson, "Expectations and Salience in White Female-African Male Self-Other Role Defiinitions" in *The Black Male in America,* D. Wilkinson and R. Taylor, ed. (Chicago: Nelson-Hall, 1977) p. 269.
7. Gary Schulman, "Race, Sex and Violence: A Laboratory Test of the Sexual Threat of the Black Male Hypothesis," *American Journal of Sociology* 79, (March 1974) pp. 1260–1277.
8. Nathan Hare, "Division and Confusion: What Happened to the Black Movement, *Black World* 25 (January 1976) pp. 20–33.
9. Carl Degler, *Neither Black Nor White* (New York: MacMillan, 1971).
10. E. Franklin Frazier, *Race and Culture Contacts in the Modern World,* (New York: Knopf, 1957) p. 335.
11. David Heer, "The Prevalence of Black/White Marriages in the United States, 1960 and 1970," *Journal of Marriage and the Family,* 36 (May 1974): 246–258.
12. Robert Staples, *The World of Black Singles,* (Westport, Connecticut: Greenwood Press), 1981.

FOOTNOTES FROM CHAPTER NINE

1. Harry Edwards, "The Draft: No equality for Blacks," *The San Francisco Examiner*, April 15, 1979, p. 3.
2. Quoted in *Jet Magazine*. June 5, 1980, p. 18.
3. "New CAVS Owner Isn't Color Blind," *The San Francisco Chronicle*, June 11, 1980, p. 63.
4. Quoted in *Civil Rights Update*, U.S. Commission on Civil Rights. September 1979, p. 1.
5. Quoted in Daniel Yankelovich, "Who Gets Ahead in America," *Psychology Today*, July 1979, p. 31.
6. "Black Youth: A Lost Generation," *Newsweek*, August 7, 1978, pp. 22–34.
7. Mark Granovetter, *Getting a Job: A Study of Contacts and Careers* (Cambridge, Mass: Harvard University Press, 1974).
8. Edwards, "The Draft. No Equality for Blacks," *The San Francisco Chronicle*, April 15, 1979, p. 3
9. Bernard Weinraub, "Military Wages War on Racism's Persistent Shadow," *The New York Times*, October 7, 1979, p. 4-E.
10. Bill Drummond, "Why Are There So Many Blacks Behind Bars in the Army," *The San Francisco Sunday Examiner and Chronicle*, This World, November 12, 1978, p. 28.
11. "Vietnam Era Veterans," *The San Francisco Sunday Examiner and Chronicle*, California Living, August 24, 1980, p. 7-12.
12. "International Probe Finds U.S. Full of Political Prisoners," *The Sun Reporter*, October 25, 1979, p. 5.
13. "A 60% Rise in Minority Prisoners," *The San Francisco Chronicle*, January 16, 1980, p. 6.
14. Robert W. Goldfarb, "Black Men — Squeezed Out by Affirmative Action," *The San Francisco Chronicle*, March 31, 1980, p. 19.
15. "Black Unemployment Higher, Survey Shows," *The San Francisco Sunday Examiner and Chronicle*, August 3, 1980, p. 2.
16. Quoted in Martin Brown, "Report Citing Black Advancement Ignores Facts," *The Michigan Daily*, March 30, 1979, p. 4.
17. Ilona Gersh, "Women Racist Affirmative Action Report," *The Militant*, April 1, 1977, p. 6.
18. "A New Racial Poll," *Newsweek*, February 26, 1979, p. 53.
19. Quoted in *Jet Magazine*, June 7, 1979, p. 32.
20. Grace Lee Boggs, "Perspectives on the Crisis of Black Youth," *Monthly Report of the Institute of the Black World*, March 1979, p. 3.
21. Chet Fuller, "A Feeling of Betrayal," *The San Francisco Chronicle*, September 7, 1978, p. 24.
22. Robert Staples, *The World of Black Singles: Changing Patterns of Male/Female Relations* (Westport, Connecticut: Greenwood Press, 1981).

FOOTNOTES FROM CHAPTER TEN

1. Nathan Hare, "Revolution without a Revolution: The Psychology of Sex and Race," *The Black Scholar* (April, 1978), 2-7.
2. Susan Brownmiller, *Against Our Will* (New York: Simon and Schuster, 1975).
3. Diana Russell, *The Politics of Rape* (New York: Stein and Day, 1975).
4. Ntozake Shange, *For Colored Girls Who Have Considered Suicide When The Rainbow is Enuf: A Choreopoem* (New York: Macmillan, 1977).
5. Michele Wallace, *Black Macho and the Myth of the Superwoman* (New York: Dial Press, 1979).
6. U.S. Bureau of the Census, *Perspectives on American Husbands and Wives*, Series p-23, No. 77, U.S. Government Printing Office, Washington, D.C. 1979.
7. Jack Horn, "Personality and Divorce," *Psychology Today*, 9 (October, 1976) p. 138.
8. James B. Stewart and Joseph W. Scott, "The Industrial Decimation of Black American Males," *Western Journal of Black Studies*, 2 (Summer 1978) 82-92.
9. Ibid.
10. Pauline Terrelonge Stone, *Feminist Consciousness and Black Women in A Feminist Perspective*, 2nd Edition, Jo Freeman, Ed., (Palo Alto, California, Mayfield, 1979) pp. 575-588.
11. Alvin Poussaint, quoted in *Jet*, January 4, 1979, p. 32.
12. Robert Staples, "To Be Young, Black and Oppressed," *The Black Scholar*, (December, 1975) 2-9.
13. Robert Staples, *The World of Black Singles: Changing Patterns of Male/Female Relationships* (Westport, Connecticut, Greenwood Press, 1981).
14. Wallace, op. cit., p. 176.
15. Leland Axelson, Jr., "The Working Wife: Differences in Perspective Among Negro and White Males," *Journal of Marriage and the Family* (August 1970) pp. 457-464; Ann Steinman and David I. Fox, "Attitudes Toward Women's Family Role Among Black and White Undergraduates," *The Family Coordinator* (October 1970) pp. 363-367.
16. Diane K. Lewis, "A Response to Inequality: Black Women, Racism and Sexism," *Signs: A Journal of Women in Culture and Society*, (Winter, 1977):339-61.
17. Cynthia F. Epstein, "Positive Effects of the Multiple Negative: Explaining the Success of Black Professional Women," *Changing Women in a Changing Society*, J. Huber, Ed. (Chicago: University of Chicago Press).
18. Daniel P. Moynihan, "The Negro Family: The Case for National Action," Washington, D.C.: U.S. Government Printing Office, 1965.
19. Cf. Robert Staples, "The Myth of the Black Matriarchy," *The Black Scholar*, (January 1970), pp. 8-16.
20. Robert L. Hampton, "Institutional Decimation, Marital Exchange and Disruption in Black Families," *Western Journal of Black Studies*, 4 (Summer 1980) : 132-139.
21. U.S. Bureau of the Census, *Divorce, Child Custody and Child Support*, Washington, D.C.: U.S. Government Printing Office, 1979.

22. Suzanne Bianchi and Reynolds Farley, "Racial Differences in Family Living Arrangements and Economic Well Being: An Analysis of Recent Trends," *Journal of Marriage and the Family*, 41 (August, 1979):537–552.
23. The National Urban League, "Inflation and the Black Consumer," Washington, D.C., National Urban League Research Department, 1974.
24. Hollie I. West, "Black America's Cassandra of the 60s Is Foretelling Doom in Race Relations in the 80s." *The Washington Post,* April 8, 1979, p. 71.

OTH   RESS:

THE $5.95
(pape   eveals
the co   rd images l   ires.

CHI   3 pp.,
ISBN   oving
collec   xist in
the st   poet's
extrac

IN T   ns for
Chil   SBN
0-933   on of
poetr   n and
deter   ghtful
repres

I'VE   a San-
chez,   s new
collec   s four
volun

FUNDERBURG LIBRARY
MANCHESTER COLLEGE

Order from: The Black Scholar Press
             P.O. Box 7106
             San Francisco, CA 94120